**Praise for UPPER MISSISSIPPI RIVER HISTORY by American Press**

"Every trip was an adventure," Larson writes. Many times when they ran aground and food supplies ran short the crew and passengers would have to wade ashore to scour the countryside for provisions.

Don Boxmeyer, *Pioneer Press*

Capt. Ron Larson combines personal observation with detail research on the Upper Mississippi River and many of the bridges, dams, river towns and steamboats. The author draws freely from historical archives to provide a wonderful collection of illustrations ⬛⬛⬛ vel.

Frit⬛

Capt. Ron Larson spent his work life as a riverboat pilot ⬛⬛⬛ way with more than a sun tan and mosquito bites. Try stories. So m⬛⬛⬛ to write them down.

John DuBois, *St. Cloud Times*

This is a well-illustrated book with interesting chapters on lock and dams, wing dams, aids to navigation, railroad bridges, rafts and rafting, the Lee-Natchez race, and paddle-wheel steamboats past and present.

James V. Swift, *Waterways Journal*

If you cruise on the Mississippi River, or if you just enjoy watching boats and barges travel up and down the river, you will enjoy this book.

Joe Hunstock, *Waterlines*

The numbered hardbound limited collector's edition of Capt. Ron's book bids well to becoming a collectors' treasure.

William C. Baker, Clinton, Iowa

**Praise for UPPER MISSISSIPPI RIVER HISTORY by British Press**

This offers a wealth of photographs and facts about the Mississippi and its famous paddle steamers, its bridges, locks, dams, log rafts and towns. The author's sometimes amusing, sometimes informative, stories from his days as a river pilot.

Josephine Jeremiah, *Waterways World*

# UPPER
# *Mississippi*
# RIVER
# HISTORY

## *Fact -- Fiction -- Legend*

### *By Captain Ron Larson, U.S.M.M., Ret.*

Capt. Ron Larson U.S.M.M.
Master / First Class Pilot

Revised Second Edition Published May, 1998
by Steamboat Press, Winona, Minnesota

First Publication - Collectors Edition - 1995
Limited-Numbered-Hard Cover, 8½x11
Library of Congress Catalog Card Number:  94-092055
ISBN:  0-9640937-0-7
List Price: $45.00

Second Edition Revised
Published May, 1998
Softbound, 7½x8½
Library of Congress Catalog Card Number:  98-60243
ISBN:  0-9640937-2-3
List Price: $18.70

Order From:  Steamboat Press
             1286 Lakeview Ave.
             Winona, MN  55987
             U.S.A.

             Ph. (507) 452-6018

Printed in United States of America

TO ALL THE RIVER PILOTS

AND CREWS I WORKED WITH

ON THE UPPER MISSISSIPPI RIVER


**RIVER PILOT'S TOAST**


HERE'S TO WIDE BRIDGES,
DEEP CHANNELS
AND NO LOCK DELAYS

## PREFACE

Being part of the river towboat industry has been a very rewarding career.

Most of the material in this book came from stories and tales of now-retired river pilots I worked with, members of the "River Boat Navy", and many river friends interested in the historical background of their river towns.

A special thank you to Wade Davick. It was his encouragement to put all these facts into a book. Lori Ness was a great help with the typing and arranging of my notes so they could be published in this book. Credit for the attractive book jacket must go to the famous Winona artist, Jim Heinlen.

Also thanks to the staff at the Murphy Library, U.W.-LaCrosse, Edwin Hill, Linda Sondreal, Paul Page, and the Winona County Historical Society and Mark Peterson for their help and contribution of many river scenes and paddlewheel steamboat pictures which made a great addition to this book.

# CONTENTS

# CONTENTS (cont.)

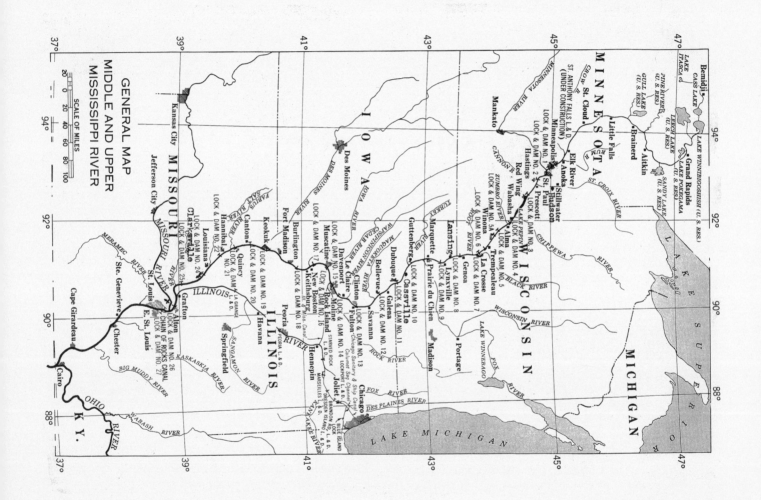

GENERAL MAP
MIDDLE AND UPPER
MISSISSIPPI RIVER

SCALE OF MILES

*Courtesy U.S. Corps of Engineers.*

## Chapter One
# *Mississippi River*

**River History, Review of Early Explorers,
and Development of the Upper Mississippi River**

*Head waters of the
Mississippi River at Lake Itasca
in northern Minnesota.
Courtesy Winona County
Historical Society.*

**M**ississippi is an American Indian name "Mech-e-sebe" translated Great River.

The first white man to have a look at the Mississippi River above its mouth at the Gulf of Mexico was a Spaniard named Hernando DeSoto in his search for a native Indian village with a large reserve of gold like the Spaniards found in Central and South America. DeSoto and the troops were making their way west when they arrived on the east bank of the Mississippi River somewhere in the area of where the city of Memphis is now located. This was in the year of 1541, forty-nine years after Columbus proved it was safe to sail east from Europe.

One hundred thirty-two years later, two Frenchmen, Louis Joliet and a Catholic priest, Jacques Marquette in 1673 were searching for a water passage to China. Leaving from a fur trader's post located at the mouth of the Fox River (which is now Green Bay, Wisconsin) in canoes with Indian guides, they traveled up the Fox River to almost its source. Then they portaged about two miles to the Wisconsin River. They went down the Wisconsin River to where it enters the Mississippi River, just south of where the city of Prairie Du Chien is now located. Joliet and Marquette canoed down the Mississippi to a point where the Arkansas River enters the Mississippi River. They then were satisfied that the River they were on (the Mississippi) entered the Gulf of Mexico and was not a water way to China. They turned back and on their return, Joliet and Marquette took the Illinois River and portaged to Lake Michigan.

*Snag boat pulling out snags that laid half sunk in the river for years causing the destruction of many boats.*
*Courtesy Winona County Historical Society.*

*Courtesy Winona Historical Society.*

In 1679, just a few years after Louis Joliet and Father Marquette returned and sent their findings to the King of France, two more Frenchmen, LaSalle and Father Hennepin, canoed down the Illinois River and started their exploration of the Mississippi River. LaSalle went down river. Father Hennepin went up river all the way to St. Anthony Falls. LaSalle took his time exploring, setting up forts and trading posts on the way. Three years later, he arrived at the mouth of the Mississippi (1682). There on the shore of the Mississippi, LaSalle claimed the Mississippi Valley Territory of France. It became known as the Louisiana Territory. The Louisiana Territory was under the rule

THE KEEL-BOAT.

*Courtesy Winona Historical Society.*

west of the Mississippi River to the United States for 15 million dollars.

Long before diesel-powered river towboats were developed, the Mississippi River served as a means of travel and the moving of freight. First, the canoe was used by the American Indians and early explorers; then the fur traders used bull boats, the pioneers used flatboats (wooden barge) and keelboats. Then came the romantic steamboats with their paddlewheels.

At first, however, because the Mississippi was a rebellious and undependable servant, river transportation had to adjust to its many changes. It was deep-flowing but turbulent during times of flood, shallow to the point of being unnavigable in times of drought, and had swift and treacherous rapids in several reaches such as at the Rock Island, Illinois, and

of the King of France for 81 years. Then in 1763 to prevent England from getting control of the Louisiana Territory, the King of France gave the territory to the King of Spain, his cousin. Thirty-seven years later (1800), through secret negotiations, Napoleon got the King of Spain to give the Louisiana Territory back to France. In 1803, Napoleon sold the Louisiana Territory

*One of the early paddlewheel steamboats. Courtesy Winona County Historical Society.*

*U.S. Army Corps of Engineers snag boat. Courtesy Winona County Historical Society.*

GIANT-SNAG - DESTROYER OF STEAMBOATS

75 Years Ago- Wednesday- November 1, 1882.
The snag puller Meigs pulled two snags out of the
Yazoo River that blocked entry into Yazoo City, Miss.
The one snag was 84 feet long and 16 feet in diameter
and the other 90 feet long and 15 feet in diameter.

SNAGS AND FIRE DESTROYED MOST STEAMBOATS

*Dredge removing a sand bar.  Courtesy Winona County Historical Society.*

*Snag Boat used to pull out snags that laid half sunk in the river for years causing the destruction of many river boats.*

UPPER MISS. RIVER IMPROVEMENT

U. S. DREDGE
WILLIAM A. THOMPSON

U. S. Engineer Office, St. Paul, Minn.
June 9, 1937.                    No. 24.

*Courtesy Winona County Historical Society.*

Keokuk, Iowa areas. Submerged rocks laid waiting for the inexperienced pilot. Every storm built up new uncharted shoals and sandbars. High winds blew hundreds of over-hanging trees into the river forming snags and deadheads which were the cause of many river pilots' undoing. Knowing this, it is easy to understand why the life of a paddlewheel steamboat on the upper Mississippi River in the early 1800's was only about three years.

The rapid growth and settlement of the Upper Midwest can be traced to the development of the river paddlewheel steamboats. These steamboats were peculiar in design and function in order to serve the particular needs of navigation and transportation on America's shallow inland rivers. Of light draft, many drawing less than eighteen inches, these paddlewheel steamboats were open and had wide decks. The boilers and engines were mounted on the main deck with the rest of the space open for cargo and cord wood that was used for fuel at first. These boats usually had a second deck (called boiler deck) for passengers and also a third deck (called Texas deck) where the crew's quarters were located. Topping the whole craft were two tall smokestacks and a twelve-by-twelve cubicle called the Pilot House. Propulsion was either by two large side paddlewheels located midship or slightly aft, or else by one large stern paddlewheel.

The first paddlewheel steamboat appeared on the Ohio and Mississippi Rivers in 1811–the "New Orleans". During the next nine years (1811-1820), sixty-three paddlewheel steamboats were built. In 1823, the paddlewheel steamboat, the "Virginia" was the first craft to ply the upper Mississippi River. In the 10-year period, 1820-1830, two hundred and three paddlewheel steamboats were built. Between 1830 to 1840, seven hundred twenty-nine more were added to the rapidly growing fleet of river paddlewheel steamboats. By 1880, over four thousand eight hundred paddlewheel steamboats had been built.

1840 to 1880 were the glory years of the paddlewheel steamboats. During this period of booming river traffic, legendary paddlewheel steamboats like the "Natchez", "Robert E. Lee", and "J.M. White", carried passengers and freight from the romantic ports of St. Louis, Memphis, Natchez, and New Orleans on the lower Mississippi River. Above St. Louis, the upper Mississippi River also became busy with river commerce as the west opened up, and immigrants came by the thousands to explore and establish homesteads, and in some cases, exploit the new territory.

The rapid growth and settlement of the Upper Midwest was because of the paddlewheel steamboat that carried the passengers and freight up and down the main artery of this nation. But by the turn of the twentieth century, the Mississippi River had lost its role as a major transportation route. The railroads had taken over, although some bulk freight was still hauled by barge, and some excursion paddlewheel steamboats

*Dynamiting rock to improve navigation in the main channel. Courtesy Winona County Historical Society.*

still plied the Mississippi River. Large numbers of the paddlewheel steamboats were gone by 1900. Of the thousands that once steamed the rivers in 1840 to 1880, fewer than three hundred were left. River men spoke of the Mississippi River as a thing of the past. The grand packets were gone, or stripped of their staterooms and made into large floating dance halls. In the excursion business, such boats as the "Capitol", "J.S. Deluxe", "Washington", "Avalon", and the "St. Paul", were all rebuilt from packet boats.

In the year, 1830, the Federal Government, aware of the upper Mississippi River's important role in the settlement of the Midwest, instructed the Army Engineers to do everything they could to improve navigation on the Ohio, Mississippi, and Missouri Rivers. First, they removed all the snags and deadheads. Then they dredged out the worst sandbars. Next they took on the reaches where there were rapids, excavating and dynamiting rock out in the channel so the rapids were safe to navigate. Then in 1878, Congress authorized the Army Engineers to build canals around the rapids at Keokuk, Iowa, and Rock Island, Illinois. In 1907, a six-foot channel was authorized by Congress. The Army Engineers accomplished this mainly by the construction of thousands of brush and rock "wing dams" which confined the river to a narrow channel during low water periods so it was deep enough for the steamboats to navigate.

In the late 1920's, it became apparent that the Upper Midwest region could greatly benefit economically from the advantage of long-haul-bulk, low-cost transportation–if a dependable channel for nine-foot draft vessels could be provided on the upper Mississippi River like the lock and dam system on the Ohio River. So, in the year 1930, Congress passed legislation that authorized the Army Corps of Engineers to build a lock and dam system on the upper Mississippi River from St. Louis, Missouri, to Minneapolis, Minnesota. Now bulk products such as grain, cement, fertilizer, chemicals, petroleum products, steel plate, iron pipe, rock salt, cottonseed, molasses, lard, L.P. gas, anhydrous ammonia in refrigerated barges, and asphalt and liquid sulfur in heated barges, are all transported in large barges–providing the Central and Upper Midwest the same economical advantages the coastal communities enjoy.

## Chapter Two
# *Paddlewheel Steamboats*

History of Early Paddlewheel Steamboats on the Mississippi River
1810 - 1855

The paddlewheel steamboat was the first steamboat on the Mississippi. Three men formed a company to build and operate a paddlewheel steamboat on the Ohio and Mississippi Rivers. Their names were Robert Fulton–who built the first successful paddlewheel steamboat-the "Clermont" which he operated on the Hudson River between New York City and Albany; Robert Livingston; and Nicholas J. Roosevelt, a Great Grand Uncle to Teddy Roosevelt.

They built their paddlewheel steamboat at Pittsburgh on the Ohio River. Construction started with the laying the keel in the summer of 1810. It was christened and launched March 17, 1811. Nicholas Roosevelt's wife christened their paddlewheel steamboat. They designed and built the paddlewheel steamboat like an ocean ship with a deep veed hull with a 34-inch diameter, low pressure condensing steam engine. It was a side paddlewheel, 116 feet long, 20 foot beam. It cost $38,000 to build the "New Orleans".

After the hull was launched, it took almost another six months to completely finish the boat and outfit it. They hired a keel boat operator, Captain Andrew Sack (Jack).

The "New Orleans" departed Pittsburgh Sept. 10,

*Str. "New Orleans". This is a picture of the replica of the first paddlewheel steamboat on the Mississippi River in 1811.*
*Built in Pittsburgh, PA. in 1911 to honor 100 years of paddlewheel steamboats on the Mississippi River.*
*115 feet long, 20 foot beam, low pressure steam engine, 34 inches in diameter with two masts for sails.*
*Courtesy Murphy Library, U. W. - LaCrosse.*

1811, with Nicholas Roosevelt, his 20-year-old wife, and crew. After stopping and showing off their new steamboat at all the towns on the Ohio River, the "New Orleans" entered the Mississippi in December of that year–1811. They managed to survive the cataclysmic disaster of the worst earthquake ever in North America on December 16, 1811, as they went past New Madrid, Missouri. For a short time, the Mississippi River ran backwards. The paddlewheel steamboat "New Orleans" arrived at the city of New Orleans, Louisiana, on January 12, 1812.

With the deep draft veed hull and low pressure condensing steam engine, the mighty Mississippi proved to be too mighty for the paddlewheel steamboat "New

Orleans". The best it could do was to reach up the Mississippi as far as Natchez, so they ended up just making trips between New Orleans and Natchez.

Then on July 14, 1814, while the "New Orleans" was tied off at Baton Rouge, the Mississippi River dropped out, and the steamboat set down on a large old stump which put a big hole in its hull. The "New Orleans" sank heeled over on its side. It was declared a complete loss. Her boiler and most of the machinery were salvaged and placed in the second paddlewheel steamboat "New Orleans".

The same year the "New Orleans" sank (1814), a flat boat pilot, Henry M. Shreve (also a shanty boat and raft pilot) started building his steamboat. His paddlewheel steamboat had a flat bottom, and he put a

*Capt. Henry Miller Shreve: His design of a river paddlewheel steamboat proved to work best on the Mississippi River. Courtesy Murphy Library, U. W.-LaCrosse.*

*Str. "Cincinnati". Cabin deck view when boat was first built - 1924. Courtesy Murphy Library, U. W. - LaCrosse*

*Str. "Northern Belle", 1856-1874, side-wheel, wood hull, built at Cincinnati, Ohio, for LaCrosse and St. Paul Co.,
226 x 29 x 5. On June 22, 1861, the Str. "Northern Belle" brought five companies of the
First Minnesota Infantry volunteers to LaCrosse, Wisc. from St. Paul, Minnesota.
Courtesy Murphy Library, U. W.-LaCrosse.*

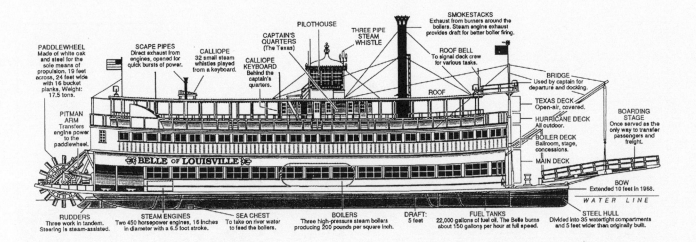

**SMOKESTACKS** Exhaust from burners around the boilers. Steam engine exhaust provides draft for better boiler firing.

**PILOTHOUSE**

**THREE PIPE STEAM WHISTLE**

**CAPTAIN'S QUARTERS** (The Texas)

**ROOF BELL** To signal deck crew for various tasks.

**CALLIOPE** 32 small steam whistles played from a keyboard.

**CALLIOPE KEYBOARD** Behind the captain's quarters.

**PADDLEWHEEL** Made of white oak and steel for the sole means of propulsion. 19 feet across, 24 feet wide with 16 bucket planks. Weight: 17.5 tons.

**SCAPE PIPES** Direct exhaust from engines, opened for quick bursts of power.

**ROOF**

**BRIDGE** Used by captain for departure and docking.

**TEXAS DECK** Open-air, covered.

**HURRICANE DECK** All outdoor.

**BOILER DECK** Ballroom, stage, concessions.

**MAIN DECK**

**BOARDING STAGE** Once served as the only way to transfer passengers and freight.

**PITMAN ARM** Transfers engine power to the paddlewheel.

BELLE OF LOUISVILLE

**BOW** Extended 10 feet in 1968.

*WATER LINE*

**RUDDERS** Three work in tandem. Steering is steam-assisted.

**STEAM ENGINES** Two 450 horsepower engines, 16 inches in diameter with a 6.5 foot stroke.

**SEA CHEST** To take on river water to feed the boilers.

**BOILERS** Three high-pressure steam boilers producing 200 pounds per square inch.

**DRAFT:** 5 feet

**FUEL TANKS** 22,000 gallons of fuel oil. The Belle burns about 150 gallons per hour at full speed.

**STEEL HULL** Divided into 35 watertight compartments and 5 feet wider than originally built.

## A BIT OF HISTORY

The Belle, built in 1914 at Pittsburgh, Pa., began life as the Idlewild, a ferry at Memphis, Tenn. A bridge across the Mississippi River killed the ferry business in 1925, and the Idlewild spent the rest of the '20s and the '30s as an excursion boat. Much of that time it was based in Louisville.

World War II brought towing duty, moving oil barges along the Ohio River.

Afterward, the boat was sold and renamed the Avalon. It tramped for excursion business throughout the Mississippi Valley. After its owners went bankrupt in 1962, the boat was sold at auction in 1962.

The buyer was Jefferson County Judge Marlow Cook. The price: $34,000.

The Belle first raced the Delta Queen on June 5, 1962. She lost, but a tradition was born.

STAFF ILLUSTRATION BY STEVE DURBIN

Source: Captain and chief engineer of the Belle of Louisville

## POWER TO THE PADDLES

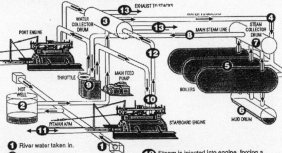

1. River water taken in.
2. Mud and solids drop out.
3. Water is pumped to a collector drum.
4. Water is sent to the three boilers.
5. Water is heated to produce steam.
6. Debris and solids settle from boilers.
7. The boilers send steam to collector drum.
8. Steam is sent to a throttle.
9. Throttle controls steam to the engines.
10. Steam is injected into engine, forcing a piston to move back and forth. A system of valves allows the engine to develop power on each forward and backward stroke.
11. Engine pushes Pitman arm back and forth to crank the paddlewheel.
12. Engine exhaust goes to collector drum to warm incoming river water.
13. Engine exhaust then goes up the main stacks, providing draft to fire the boilers.

## THE PILOTHOUSE

STAFF PHOTO BY KEITH WILLIAMS

1. Pilot wheel.
2. Pilothouse to engine room telegraph.
3. Power steering levers.
4. Pilot wheel brake pedals. (To stop wheel and hold rudder position)
5. Old three-bell telegraph to engine room.
6. Intercom systems and main electrical control panel
7. Starboard searchlight control
8. Port searchlight control
9. Steam whistle foot pedal
10. Communications: 2 marine radios, 1 cellular phone and 1 phone to crew
11. Trumpet (Bell sound returns from engine room).

*PADDLEWHEEL STEAMBOAT*
*Illustration*
*Courtesy "Belle of Louisiana" Operating Board.*

*This is a good view of a paddlewheel steamboat engine room.  Courtesy Winona County Historical Society.*

*Str. "Gadie Eastman". This is a good example of the early steamboats of the 1830ís.*
*Courtesy Winona County Historical Society.*

high pressure steam engine in this steamboat. He put the steam engine and boiler on the main deck, and then he built a second deck over that and put his pilot house up on top of that. As he was building the steamboat, people would come down to the levee to look at his steamboat. They would look at it and shake their heads and say, "Henry, when you put your steamboat in the river, it will tip over". But Henry knew what he was doing. He named his paddlewheel steamboat, the "Washington" after our first president. Then in the spring of 1815, Henry Shreve left Louisville, Kentucky, with his paddlewheel steamboat, the "Washington", went down the Ohio, entered the Mississippi at Cairo, Illinois, went all the way down to New Orleans, Louisiana, and returned to Louisville. He made that round trip in 45 days. Before that, a round trip from Louisville to New Orleans by keelboat took 4 to 5 months.

The design of the paddlewheel steamboat, "Washington" proved to be the best for the river. The river steamboats for the next 100 years followed Henry Shreve's basic design, with flat bottom hulls, and the pilot house on top to provide 360 degrees visibility for the pilot.

Side paddlewheels were used on the first steamboats. Because the side paddlewheels had to be outside of the hull, the hull was narrow and had a draft of 4 to 6 feet. So in the early years, this limited them to the waters of the lower Mississippi and Ohio Rivers.

Putting the paddlewheel on the stern solved this problem. The hull could be wider. Some of the small stern paddlewheel steamboats had a draft of only 18 inches.

The main deck or lower deck contained boilers, steam engines, fuel, and freight. The second deck was called boiler deck because it was over the boiler. This was for passenger use. This was the main cabin with its stateroom on each side. Down the center of the main cabin, meals were served. It was also used for dancing, social events, and card playing. Ladies' cabins were always to the aft of the main cabin. Kitchen and washrooms were adjacent to the side paddlewheel houses. The third deck was called hurricane deck. The fourth deck–the deck above the skylight windows of the main cabin was called the Texas deck. This deck was used for crews' quarters. This was so named because Texas became a state about the same time this deck came into use. Steamboats named their rooms after different states instead of numbering them. This is where the term "stateroom" got started.

At first, the early paddlewheel steamboats were crude and ungainly. The early ones were under 100 feet in length, only about 50 to 70 feet with a beam of 12 to 18 feet wide.

Sleeping accommodations consisted of rows of open bunk berths with mattresses made of hay or corn husks which were separated by curtains. Enclosed staterooms didn't come into use in the main cabin

*This is a typical early paddlewheel steamboat. Courtesy Winona County Historical Society.*

deck until the mid 1840's. At first, the staterooms were only about six feet square. It wasn't until after the Civil War, about 1880, that the staterooms were built of any size and had regular beds instead of bunk berths.

Illumination was by candle or kerosene lamp in the early years. After the Civil War, gas lamps came into use. Electricity was introduced in the late 1870's–chiefly for searchlights. Electric interior lighting did not come into common use on paddlewheel

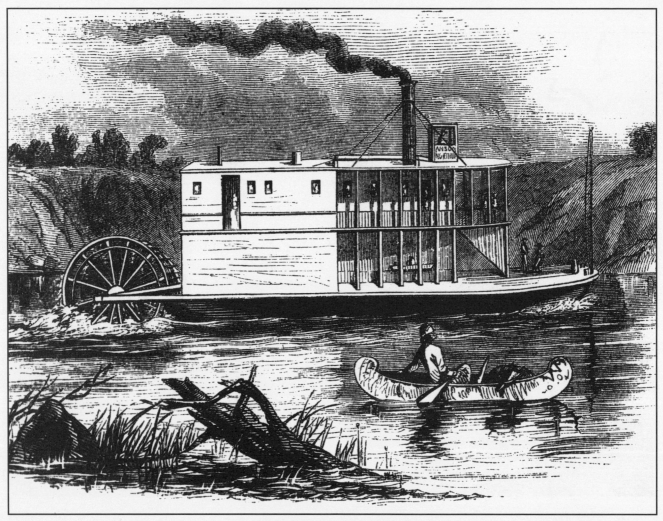

*Str. "Anson Northrup", a good example of the early paddlewheel steamboats. They were very basic.
Courtesy Winona County Historical Society.*

*Str. "Grand Republic", 1867-1877, wood hull, side-wheel, built in Shousetown, Pa.*
*First named "Great Republic", 335 x 51 x 9.5, compound steam engines, 28 and 56 inches in diameter with a 10 foot stroke,*
*6 boilers. By 1871, the first owners went bankrupt. New owners had hull lengthened to 350 ft. and widened the guards,*
*so the overall width was increased to 56 feet. Also outfitted it so it was the most luxurious boat on the river.*
*Name was changed to "Grand Republic". In 1877, it was destroyed by fire. Courtesy Winona County Historical Society.*

steamboats until around 1900. Hot and cold running water and water closets did not appear until after the Civil War. The early paddlewheel steamboats were more of a floating bath house or barracks. But at that time in history, it was superior to any type of overland travel. Stage coach and wagon on rough roads was far from comfortable.

The early paddlewheel steamboats did not have the highly publicized luxuries of the so-called floating palaces. Inadequate accommodations and poor food were the rule rather than the exception. There was rude manners among crew and passengers. Inadequate ventilation and noisy vibrations from the steam engine were distractions to reading, conversation, and sleeping. In the summer, heat from the boiler was a serious discomfort when trying to sleep. During crowded trips, standards of service deteriorated, and meals had to be served in shifts.

At first on the early paddlewheel steamboats, meals were of the "pork and beans" fare. Cabin passengers and officers sat at a long table set up in the main cabin, while deck hands, boiler firemen, and deck passengers ate wherever they could. Quality sometimes was poor because of unskilled chefs.

After the Civil War, cookery equaled or excelled that of the finest restaurants and hotels. Menus featured a wide variety of meats, followed by potatoes, corn and other vegetables. Wine and spirits were principal drinks with meals. Lack of water clarification made drinking water from the river questionable.

Accommodations for deck passengers usually were nonexistent. Even soft spots among the cargo were at a premium for sleeping. Deckers usually brought their own food and utensils. Food was chosen for durability. Deckers could obtain a slight reduction in fare if they agreed to work with the deck crew, principally in wood loading operation.

Fares in the 1850's one way between New Orleans and St. Louis were $15.00 for cabin passage and only $3.00 for deck passage. After 1880, fares were based on 3 cents a mile including meals. One way fare from St. Paul to St. Louis was $21.00. It was almost cheaper to ride a steamboat than to stay at home.

Wood was used for fuel at first. The paddlewheel steamboats made a practice to stop twice a day at established woodyards. They burned 20 to 30 cords of wood a day. By 1840, they started using coal because wood along the rivers started to be in short supply. By 1880, along the Ohio River, all the paddlewheel steamboats used coal. Wood sold for $1.50 to $3.00 a cord.

Before the lock and dams were built, navigation depended on the weather conditions. Spring rains and snow melt were looked upon as favorable conditions. Wet seasons meant periods of unrestricted operation of the river paddlewheel steamboats. Low-water condition periods began in June, and the rivers went up and down until the fall rainy season. Then in late

*Str. "Eclipse" (lower Mississippi River luxury boat) 1853-1860, wood hull, side-wheel, 363 x 40 x 9.*
*Main cabin was 330 feet long (largest side paddlewheel steamboat built).  Steam engines 36 inches in*
*diameter with an 11 foot stroke.  Paddlewheels 40 feet in diameter working 15 foot buckets.*
*Width of boat including guards was 77 feet, smoke stacks 85 inches in diameter, 95 feet high.*
*Crew of 121:  70 firemen, 25 stewards and waiters, 5 cooks, 3 mates, 6 deck hands, 5 engineers, 5 clerks,*
*2 pilots, master and owner, Capt. Edward T. Sturgeon.  On Feb. 21, 1860, it was badly damaged in a storm.*
*It was towed to Memphis, Tenn. and used as a wharfboat until dismantled.  Courtesy Murphy Library, U. W.-LaCrosse.*

*This is the way the paddlewheel steamboats carried the cord wood. They would burn 20 to 30 cords of wood a day.*
*Courtesy Winona County Historical Society.*

*Str. "J.M. White" 1878-1886, wood hull, side-wheel, built at Jefferson, Ind. 312 x 47.9 x 11.5, steam engines 43 inches in diameter with an 11 foot stroke, 10 boilers. Paddlewheels 44 feet in diameter working 18.5 foot buckets, smoke stacks 80 feet high. Length overall 321 feet, width including guards 91 ft., main cabin 19 ft. wide, 233 ft. long. State rooms 8 x 10, 9 x 12, 9 x 14, and two bridal suites 12 x 14. On Dec. 13, 1886, it exploded and burned at Point Coupee Parish, La. Courtesy Jim Heinlen.*

November, winter set in and navigation closed down.

On the upper Mississippi, depth varied from 3 feet at St. Paul to 5 feet at Cairo. The shifting and changing of the channel, new sandbars and islands, and older ones washed away made every river trip an adventure. During low-water periods, there were delays caused by groundings and sandbars. Paddlewheel steamboats would have to just wait for it to rain enough to raise the

*This is a good view of jigsaw carpentry (steamboat gothic) in the cabin deck lounge of the Str. "Grand Republic".*
*Courtesy Murphy Library, U. W.-LaCrosse.*

river enough to get off ground or over the sandbar. Sometimes that would take just a few days, and other times, it would take a week or two. If food supplies ran out during the delay, passengers and crew had to go ashore and search the countryside for food.

The Golden Age of the river paddlewheel steamboats was from 1840 to 1862–the decade before the Civil War. They had fine furniture, crystal chandeliers,

*Pilot house view of the paddlewheel steamboat, "Capitol".*
*Courtesy Murphy Library, U. W-LaCrosse.*

thick carpeting, and large mirrors, exquisite china, shining silverware, and sparkling cut glass.

Lower Mississippi paddlewheel steamboats were over 300 feet in length. The "Grand Republic" and the "Eclipse" were 365 feet in length. They cost $400,000 to build. It was said the river paddlewheel steamboats were "expensive jigsaw carpentry (steamboat gothic) with a steam engine on a raft". They had gaudy paint-

*Getting a contract to transport mail was sought for by all the Packet Boat companies.
It was a good source of additional income. Courtesy Winona County Historical Society.*

ed paddlewheel houses, feathered chimney tops and elaborately carved decorations on the pilot house and cabin interiors.

Most of the paddlewheel steamboats were built on the Ohio River. From 1820 to 1880, The Ohio River Boat Yards built 6,000 paddlewheel steamboats.

In the beginning, when laying at a landing, and the steam engines stopped, adequate water supply to the boiler was a vexing problem because the steam engines also pumped fresh water into the boilers. Steam pressure continuing to build created a safety hazard. To solve this, a small auxiliary steam engine was added to provide water to the boilers. This was called the doctor engine. It was also used to pump bilges as well. In 1850, the use of unexpandable cast iron boilers and steampipes was discontinued in favor of the more flexible wrought iron and copper.

Paddlewheels adapted well to shallow river channels. They survived the punishment of snags, deadheads, and sandbars. Damage repairs were readily made by the crew, which at times was almost a nightly chore.

Moving the side paddlewheel from midship to about two thirds of the distance aft came about in 1840. This greatly increased the efficiency of the side paddlewheelers. Because the bucket (paddle) caught the down side of the hull wave, there was very little power wasted lifting water.

The most elegant and beautiful paddlewheel steamboats were the "Grand Republic", "J.M. White", "Natchez", and "Robert E. Lee". The "J.M. White", a side paddlewheel steamboat, was built in 1878. Her dimensions were 312 feet, 7 inches in length with a 47 feet, 9 inch beam. The "J.M. White" was probably the fastest paddlewheel steamboat on the Mississippi River. Captain John W. Tobin was her master.

The "J.M. White" had elaborate jigsaw carpentry (steamboat gothic), fancy lettering, and tall chimneys with ornamental feathers on top. The pilot house looked like a gazebo. The climax of the "steamboat gothic" splendor was achieved in the main cabin or grand saloon as it was called–befitting its social function as the center place of paddlewheel steamboat life.

On each side of the grand saloon were rows of elegant state rooms. Overhead were stained glass windows. The ceiling was supported by ornate columns and connecting arches carved in lacelike patterns. The aft end of the main cabin which was reserved for the ladies, had a huge mirror. This created the illusion of doubling the grand saloon's length, which was almost 200 feet long to begin with. The grand saloon was carpeted with rich thick Brussels carpeting and illuminated by crystal chandeliers equipped with gas lamps. The walls were paneled in walnut or rosewood. Handsome upholstered and hand-carved furniture was used throughout the grand saloon. There was a grand piano and a large silver water cooler with silver drink-

*One of the paddlewheel steamboats that were built after the Civil War.*
*Courtesy Winona County Historical Society.*

ing cups chained to its sides.

The "J.M. White" operated on the Mississippi River only eight years. On December 13, 1886, near Bayou Sara, Louisiana, fire broke out near the boilers on main deck. It all went up in smoke and flames. In a very short time, it burnt down to the water line and sank.

River paddlewheel steamboats operated with around thirty crew members: a master, 2 pilots, a chief engineer, 2 assistant engineers, 2 oilers, 2 firemen, 8 deck hands, 2 mates, a radio operator, a purser, a mud clerk, 2 cooks, a cabin boy, 2 waitresses, a laundress, and a watchman.

On paddlewheel steamboats, the captain was the master, sometimes called roof captain. He had dominion over the passengers, deck, and engineer crews. The mate was the captain's deputy. He was in charge of the deck hands (called "roosters"), and supervised all repair work, storage of cargo and livestock, and the loading of fuel. The pilot reigned supreme in the pilot house. A good pilot was paid a very good wage.

The purser kept all the records, assigned the passengers to their staterooms, collected the fares and freight charges, and took care of all passenger's complaints. The mud clerk assisted the purser, and at each landing, went ashore and checked on all freight to be picked up and dropped off. He also negotiated with the wood yard owners on the price of the cord wood.

At first, paddlewheel steamboat justice was administered by a court of passengers. But later, the captain was usually called to enforce and interpret the rules of conduct. Serious infractions like theft, swindling, illicit sex, prostitution, and murder were handled by turning the offender over to authorities at the next landing or by stranding them on a sandbar in the middle of the river.

Rules against gambling were generally ignored. Stewards were willing to provide card tables and decks of cards for poker games. The stewards were hired by professional gamblers to make certain that every "new" deck of cards was a marked one. River paddlewheel steamboats were favorite operations for professional gamblers because they furnished a continuous parade of wealthy planters and merchants that would sit down to play a friendly game to pass the time.

Congress passed the Steamboat Act in 1852. It was to correct the unsatisfactory conditions on river paddlewheel steamboats. It required installation of proper gauges and safety devices on steam boilers, also a licensing system for steam engineers and river pilots. But very little was done to enforce them until better regulation and enforcement procedures were passed by Congress in 1871.

From 1823 to 1863, 360 paddlewheel steamboats worked on the upper Mississippi River from St. Louis to St. Paul. Seventy-two were lost: 38 hit snags or

*Str. "Quincy" on July 11, 1906, hit a snag in the river just above Trempealeau, Wisc. It sank close enough to shore so all passengers could get off safely. A special train was sent to take the passengers on to their destinations. The boat was raised and later sold. Courtesy Winona County Historical Society.*

deadheads and sank, 10 burned, 3 hit bridge piers and sank or burned, 3 were lost in the Civil War, 1 was destroyed in a tornado, and 2 by boiler explosion.

The worst marine disaster in maritime history happened on the Mississippi River just above Memphis, Tennessee. The paddlewheel steamboat, "Sultana", had two thousand five hundred troops on their way home after being held prisoner by the Confederate Army down south. The paddlewheel steamboat "Sultana's" boiler exploded. The steamboat caught fire and was completely destroyed. One thousand five hundred and forty-seven soldiers died plus many of the crew. This disaster happened April 27, 1865, the same day Abraham Lincoln was assassinated.

*Courtesy Winona County Historical Society.*

*Courtesy Winona County Historical Society.*

## Chapter Three
# *Railroad Bridges Across the Mississippi*

Rock Island R.R. Bridge, Winona and St. Peter R.R. Bridge, Eads R.R. and Hyway Bridge

At the time of this writing, there are 169 bridges across the Mississippi River: 122 highway bridges, 34 railroad bridges, 12 highway-railroad combination bridges, and one pipeline bridge.

In the 1800's, Congress passed a law that required any bridge that could not be opened (to allow boats to pass) to be built high enough to provide a minimum of 52 feet of clearance at high water.

The first railroad bridge to be built across the Mississippi River was built in 1855-56. It was a wooden trestle bridge with a swing span that would open to let the paddlewheel steamboats pass. It crossed the Mississippi River from Rock Island, Illinois, to Davenport, Iowa, just below the Rock Island Rapids. The first train to go across crossed on April 21, 1856. They had a big celebration on both sides of the river that day. The president of the railroad was there. Governors from both states and mayors from both towns were also there. Bands played, speeches were given by the dignitaries, and a big parade was held.

Fifteen days later–May 4, 1856–the side paddlewheel steamboat, "Effie Afton", after stopping at Davenport, Iowa, and off loading freight and passengers, got under way and started up river. The railroad

*Floating railroad bridge on the Mississippi River between Prairie Du Chien, Wisc., and North McGregor, Iowa.*
*Courtesy Winona County Historical Society.*

swing span swung open and the "Effie Afton" passed through. As the "Effie Afton" started up through the Rock Island Rapids, the starboard paddlewheel shaft broke. The "Effie Afton" floated back down and crashed against the railroad bridge. "Effie Afton's" smokestacks fell over. The wood-burning cook stove in the galley tipped over. The boat caught on fire. So did the railroad bridge. Hundreds of small skiffs and a

*Str. "Gray Eagle", 1857-1861, wood hull, side-wheel, built at Cincinnati, Ohio, for Minnesota Packet Company.
250 x 35 x 5, steam engines 22 inches in diameter with a 7 foot stroke, 4 boilers. On May 9, 1861,
it hit the Rock Island Railroad Bridge and sank. Courtesy Murphy Library, U. W-LaCrosse.*

local ferryboat rushed to rescue the passengers and crew. Three hundred oxen on the main deck jumped into the river. The "Effie Afton" burned and sank. But not a single passenger or crew was lost. It took almost a week before all the oxen that had jumped in the river could be rounded up.

The Captain, owner of the "Effie Afton", filed suit against the railroad for damages to his boat and also sued to prevent the railroad from building any bridges across the Mississippi River declaring them a navigation hazard. But the railroad won out. The lawyer that represented the railroad in that case was Abraham Lincoln.

In 1866, the U.S. Coast Guard did declare the Rock Island Railroad Bridge a navigation hazard. The river pilots called it "Gate of Death". Captain Smith Harris of the Eagle Packet Boat Company hit the Rock Island Railroad Bridge with the "Gray Eagle" and sank. Because of that accident, he gave up piloting paddlewheel steamboats.

It wasn't until 1872 that a new bridge was built–about a mile further down river from the lower end of the Rock Island Rapids, and the old railroad bridge was removed. Then in 1894, the railroad bridge was replaced with a riveted steel combination bridge for both rail and autos.

*High winds caused the paddlewheel steamboat to strike the lower Winona Railroad Bridge June 13, 1915. Captain William York was able to get the boat into shallow water below the bridge so only the bow went under. The steamboat, "Hill" brought the passengers back to Winona. The "Frontenac" was raised, repaired, and was back on the river in a couple weeks. Courtesy Winona County Historical Society.*

*The paddlewheel steamboat "Frontenac" after it was raised and put back into service. Courtesy Winona County Historical Society.*

The Winona and St. Peter Railroad at Winona, Minnesota, also built a bridge across the Mississippi River. The decision to build and extend their railroad east into Wisconsin was made in 1870. A contractor agreed to build a railroad bridge for the Winona and St. Peter for $250,000. Construction got started in late summer, and by May 26, 1871, the Winona and St. Peter Railroad had a wooden trestle bridge across the Mississippi River with a swing span that would open to allow steamboats to pass. On May 26th, they had a big celebration. After all the speeches, the city band played, and the last spike was driven to complete connecting the East with the West.

The next day, the first train to cross over the new bridge was parked waiting for the bridge tender to come back from lunch. When the bridge tender saw

EADS BRIDGE, ACROSS THE MISSISSIPPI, AT ST. LOUIS, MO.                    125

*Eads Bridge at St. Louis, Mo. First riveted steel trussed bridge ever built. Courtesy Winona County Historical Society.*

the train waiting, he ran down to the river bank, jumped into his rowboat, and hurriedly rowed his boat out to the swing span that was open to let any paddle-wheel steamboats through while the bridge tender was off for lunch. The bridge tender was very excited–his first train. He didn't want to delay it any longer. He got to the swing span, tied off his rowboat, climbed up, stoked up the fire in the boiler, got up steam, and

*Str. "Dubuque" coming through the Dubuque Railroad bridge at Dubuque, Iowa. Courtesy Winona County Historical Society.*

began to swing the bridge closed. He signalled the train to cross. In his haste he forgot to recouple the tracks. Luckily the locomotive somehow made it across. But the flatbed railcars, loaded with quarry stone, snagged on the unaligned rails and plunged into the river, taking the swing span of the bridge, and the bridge tender with them. It wasn't until the next year (1872) that the repairs were complete, and the Winona and St. Peter Railroad could start using their bridge.

In 1882, the Winona and St. Peter Railroad was

bought by the Chicago Northwestern, and they replaced the wooded trestle bridge with a riveted steel bridge.

The first railroad bridge to cross the Mississippi River at St. Louis, Missouri, was built in the years 1867 to 1874. Seven years it took to complete, and it is still in use today. It is a combination bridge: the upper deck being used by cars and trucks, the lower deck used for trains. The cost was 9 million dollars. It is named after the man that designed and built it: Mr. Eads. The Eads Bridge is over a mile long–six thousand, two hundred and twenty feet in length and fifty-four feet wide. The Eads Bridge was the first riveted steel trussed bridge ever built. Both east and west stone piers are set in bedrock. The west pier goes down ninety-one feet, and the east pier goes down one hundred and twenty-seven feet. Fourteen men lost their lives in the construction of the Eads Bridge.

Before there was radio communication between the railroad bridges and the river towboats, there was always some anxious moments for the river pilot, wondering if the bridge would open in time. It is true that by law, the towboat had priority over the trains. But the bridge tender of the bridge was on the railroad payroll, so that priority wasn't much help.

As the pilot was bringing his fifteen barge tow down the river–to be sure he had room to stop his tow–when a good mile above the railroad bridge, he would blow one loud long blast on his whistle. This used to be the signal to request the bridge be opened. Then he waited, hoping the bridge tender was awake, especially if it was 3 o'clock in the morning. When the bridge tender heard the towboat's whistle, he would check to see if there was a train close by. The bridge tender would blow his whistle to indicate whether he could open or not. If he could start to open, the bridge tender would blow one long whistle. If he had to wait for a train to cross first, he would blow four short whistles. Now the whistle on the railroad bridge was not very loud, more like a car horn, and if the wind was blowing away from the towboat, usually the pilot never heard the bridge tender's whistle. But there was a good visual signal that Mother Nature provided. All the railroad bridges provided good nesting places for barn pigeons. When the bridge tender started to open the swing span of the bridge, usually 50 to 100 or more pigeons would take to the air. The towboat pilot would see this, give a good sigh of relief, and start to ease his tow down to the bridge, and hopefully pass through between the bridge piers without breaking anything.

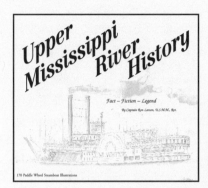

## Chapter Four
# *Great Paddlewheel Steamboat Race of 1870*

Race from New Orleans to St. Louis between the "Natchez" and the "Robert E. Lee"

*The Victory Bowl Trophy won by the Str. "Robert E. Lee" and Capt. John W. Cannon. Courtesy Murphy Library, U. W.-LaCrosse.*

C aptain Leathers, owner and master of the "Natchez" and Captain Cannon, owner and master of the "Robert E. Lee" were competitors in the New Orleans and St. Louis passenger and freight business on the Mississippi River. Everyone along the Mississippi River from New Orleans to St. Louis knew that someday both paddlewheel steamboats would be leaving New Orleans the same day. This could only lead to a paddlewheel steamboat race. The two paddlewheel steamboats were about evenly matched. The year was 1870. In the last part of the month of June, both the "Robert E. Lee" and the "Natchez" were in New Orleans getting ready to depart for St. Louis. Newspapers up and down the Mississippi River started printing stories suggesting there would be a paddlewheel steamboat race. Then in the evening of June 30, 1870, at 5:00 p.m. sharp, the paddlewheel steamboat, "Robert E. Lee" backed away from the New Orleans levee and started up the river. Four minutes later, the paddlewheel steamboat, "Natchez", departed New Orleans. The great paddle-

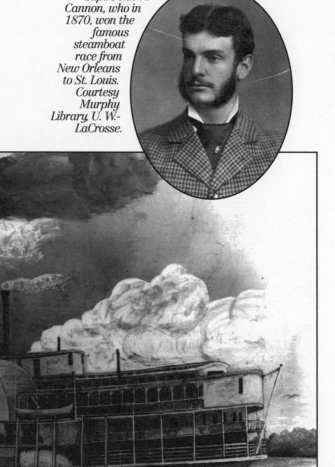

*Capt. John W. Cannon, who in 1870, won the famous steamboat race from New Orleans to St. Louis. Courtesy Murphy Library, U. W.-LaCrosse.*

*Str. "Robert E. Lee" 1866-1876, wood hull, side-wheel, built at Albany, Ind. 285 x 46 x 9, steam engines 40 inches in diameter with a 10 foot stroke, 8 boilers. Courtesy Murphy Library, U. W.-LaCrosse.*

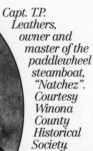

*Capt. T.P. Leathers, owner and master of the paddlewheel steamboat, "Natchez". Courtesy Winona County Historical Society.*

wheel steamboat race was on. At first, the "Robert E. Lee" drew steadily away from the "Natchez". The "Natchez" had a leak in a steam line. So the "Natchez" had to run slow until it was repaired. After the engineers had made a temporary repair on that leaking steam line, the "Natchez" started to gain on the "Robert E. Lee". The paddlewheel steamboats arrived at Vicksburg, Mississippi, early in the evening

*Str. "Natchez" 1869-1881, wood hull, side-wheel, built at Cincinnati, Ohio. 301 x 46.6 x 9.8, steam engines 34 inches in diameter with a 10 foot stroke, 8 boilers. It was stranded on a sand bar near Rising Sun, Ind., June 1879. By July 13, a rise in the river made it possible to pull it off. It was towed to Cincinnati and tied off there. In 1881, it was towed to Jeffersonville, Ind. and dismantled. Courtesy Murphy Library, U. W.-LaCrosse.*

*Str. "Robert E. Lee" and the Str. "Natchez" in the New Orleans to St. Louis race in 1870. Courtesy Winona County Historical Society.*

*Str. "Sucker State" 1860-1867, wood hull, side-wheel, built at Pittsburgh, Pa. 230 x 36 x 5.5, steam engines 22 inches in diameter with a 7 foot stroke. It was destroyed by fire in Alton Slough, June 1867. Str. "Sucker State" was a sister boat to the Str. "Hawkeye State" that holds the record time between St. Louis, Mo. and St. Paul, Minn. Courtesy Winona County Historical Society.*

the next day–July 1st. Vicksburg is a little over 300 miles above New Orleans. It was an ideal fueling stop for the paddlewheel steamboats. Here is where Captain Cannon on the "Robert E. Lee" played his trump card. He had made provisions to have the paddlewheel steamboat, "Frank Pargoud", come out and meet the "Robert E. Lee" with a load of fuel-including about one hundred tons of pine knots, and stay along side as the "Robert E. Lee" kept right on going up the Mississippi River as the fuel was put on board. By the time the boats passed Memphis, Tennessee, the "Robert E. Lee" still had a full hour lead on the "Natchez".

Both captains had made arrangements with the farmers and merchants along the river to round up all the ham and bacon fat they could find to burn in their boilers. For hours after the steamboats went by, it smelled like someone was frying bacon all along the river. Then early in the evening, July 3rd, above Cairo, Illinois, thick fog set in. The steam line that the engineers had done a temporary repair on was acting up again on the "Natchez". Captain Leathers, hoping the fog was so thick that Captain Cannon on the "Robert E. Lee" would tie off, decided to chance it and tied off so the engineers could replace that leaky steam line. But Captain Cannon ran the "Robert E. Lee" on a slow bell in the fog. When the fog lifted, the "Robert E. Lee" had a good lead on the "Natchez" again and reached St. Louis, Missouri at 11:25 a.m. on July 4th, 1870. The "Robert E. Lee" made the 1218

mile run from New Orleans to St. Louis in 3 days, 18 hours and 14 minutes. Six hours later, the "Natchez" arrived.

The fastest time between St. Louis, Missouri, and St. Paul, Minnesota, is held by the paddlewheel steamboat, "Hawkeye State": two days, twenty-one hours and forty-nine minutes. The "Hawkeye State" made that run in 1868 before the lock and dams were put in so that record still stands today.

# Chapter Five
# *Log Rafts on the Upper Mississippi*

First Log Raft on the Upper Mississippi River,
Rafting Across Lake St. Croix and Lake Pepin,
First Paddlewheel Steamboat to Tow Log Rafts on the Mississippi River,
Chippewa Log Boom

After the Civil War, they started moving log rafts with paddlewheel steamboats. But before that, raft men steered the log rafts with long sweeps (oars) and just floated down the river with the current.

Steve Hanks, a farmer near Albany, Illinois, was the first log raft man to take a raft of logs down the Mississippi River. He just happened to be in the right place at the right time, and was smart enough to take advantage of the opportunity. Steve raised beef cattle on his farm. He made a big sale of his herd of beef to a logging camp up in northwestern Wisconsin. But to make the sale, he had to deliver the cattle to the logging camp. With the help of a few neighboring farmers, they drove the herd of beef cattle up to the logging camp in the late fall–after all the crops were in. Then they all stayed there that winter working in that logging camp.

In the spring of 1844, all the logs they cut that winter were rolled into the St. Croix River and floated down to a sawmill at Marine, Minnesota. There the logs were caught and held in a holding basin (called a boom site) until they could be dragged out and up on shore. While there were still many logs in that holding basin, there was a flash flood and quite a few of the logs broke loose and went down the St. Croix River into Lake St. Croix. The only way they had to get the

*Log raft being guided down the upper Mississippi River by raftmen. Courtesy Murphy Library, U. W.-LaCrosse.*

logs back up to the sawmill was to drag them out of the lake and bring them back over land with oxen. It was decided it wasn't worth the effort.

Steve Hanks knew that if he could round up those logs and make them into a raft, then float them down the Mississippi to St. Louis, the sawmill there would pay him a good price for those logs. So he made a deal with the sawmill at Marine on the St. Croix and bought those logs at a very reasonable price with the money he had from the sale of his beef cattle. With the help of his neighboring farmers that helped him bring the beef up to the logging camp, he rounded up all those runaway logs. He made them into a raft 600 feet long. With his neighbors' help, Steve got the log

*Building a log raft at a boom site with long sweeps (oars) to steer the raft before the use of a paddlewheel steamboat.*
*Courtesy Winona County Historical Society*

*A large raft of logs going down the river with the aid of a paddlewheel steamboat. Courtesy Winona County Historical Society.*

raft down the St. Croix River into the Mississippi, and 30 days later, the log raft arrived at the sawmill in St. Louis. After that, because this was so successful, Steve Hanks spent more time taking rafts of logs down the river than he did farming.

**Rafting across a lake**

Rafts of logs coming out of northwestern Wisconsin had to cross two lakes: Lake St. Croix and Lake Pepin. Since there was no current in the lake, the raftmen had to find a way to get their log rafts across. At first, the raftmen used a long rope about 1000 feet in length and a heavy anchor. They put the anchor in a

*Steamboat rafter "J. W. Van Sant" taking a log raft down the river. Notice the line going from the log raft to a mid-ship capstan on the steamboat to help steer the log raft around the bends in the river. Courtesy Winona County Historical Society.*

*Sam Van Sant, designed and built the first successful paddlewheel steamboat to move log rafts down the river. In 1892, he was elected Governor of the state of Minnesota. Courtesy Winona County Historical Society.*

skiff, rowed the skiff out ahead of the log raft as far as the rope would let them, and dropped the anchor overboard. Then the crew on the raft started to pull on the anchor rope. When they got the raft of logs up to where the anchor was, they pulled the anchor up, put it in the skiff, and started all over again. They kept this up until they had the log raft across the lake and into the river. Pulling the log raft across the lake was very heavy, back-breaking work. This led to the use of a team of horses on the log raft to pull on the anchor rope. With the use of horses, they had to provide a smooth surface. The raftmen accomplished this by laying slabboards on the logs. Eventually, the raftmen started using a steamboat to tow the log raft across the lakes–St. Croix and Pepin. Using a steamboat to push the log rafts down the river didn't come about until after the Civil War when Sam Van Sant at LeClair, Iowa, rigged his steamboat with midship capstan, so he could steer the log rafts around the bends in the river.

### Log Raftman Poem

I see you are a raftman, sir
and not a common bum.
For no one but a raftman
stirs his coffee with his thumb.

(Author unknown)

Somewhere around 1860, the paddlewheel steamboat, "Union", tried to push a log raft down the Mississippi River from Lake Pepin. But it had so much trouble trying to get the log raft around the bends, it gave up the idea before it got to Alma, Wisconsin. Sam Van Sant–down at LeClaire, Iowa –after hearing about the trouble the paddle-wheel steamboat, "Union", had, designed a stern paddlewheel steamboat with two steam-powered midship capstans located on both port and starboard sides of the boat. He called them steam niggers. This made it possible to change the alignment of the paddlewheel steamboat from straight to an angle either port or starboard to twist the log raft around the bends in the river.

*Some rafts going down the river were made up of sawed lumber. Courtesy Winona County Historical Society.*

*One of Sam Van Santís paddlewheel steamboats steering a raft of logs down the upper Mississippi River.*
*Courtesy Murphy Library, U. W.-LaCrosse.*

Sam Van Sant came back home from the Army to LeClaire, Iowa, after the Civil War. He joined his dad in his boatyard repairing paddlewheel steamboats. During the winter of 1865, he talked all their carpenters into working for deferred wages to build a stern paddlewheel steamboat with his idea of steam niggers. Then he went to Cincinnati, Ohio, and talked a steam engine company into building him a steam engine and steam capstan on credit. He got his boat built and waited for the steam engines to be delivered. It was

*Str. "J. W. Van Sant", the first paddlewheel steamboat built to successfully steer log rafts down the Mississippi River.*
*Courtesy Winona County Historical Society.*

spring before they arrived, and they arrived across the river from LeClaire, Iowa, at Byron, Illinois. He couldn't get anyone to take on the job of hauling them across the ice because it had already started to melt. He had to get those steam engines across somehow and get them installed in the boat, and have it ready to go as soon as the river opened up. The boat had to

earn the money Sam needed to pay the bills coming due, or he and his dad would lose everything they owned. He built a very large sled to distribute the weight of the heavy steam engines over a large surface of ice. Then he took a fifty foot log chain and hitched his horse to the end of the chain. This way he felt if the horse broke through the ice, the horse would be far enough ahead that the sled with the steam engines would still be on good ice, and he could get the steam engines back to the shore. Everything worked out fine. Sam got his steam engines across the river and into his new stern paddlewheel steamboat, "J.W. Van Sant". As soon as the Mississippi River opened up, Sam Van Sant got a contract from Weyerhauser, who at that time, had a sawmill at Rock Island, Illinois, to move a log raft of Weyerhauser's that was caught frozen in ice at Clinton, Iowa, to the sawmill at Rock Island. That went so well and so impressed Mr. Weyerhauser that he gave Sam Van Sant the job of bringing all his log rafts down from the boom site at Beef Slough, located just above Alma, Wisconsin, to Rock Island, Illinois.

As soon as Sam Van Sant had paid off all his creditors, he built another boat. In 1883, he moved his company to Winona, Minnesota, and was operating a fleet of stern paddlewheel steamboats, moving log rafts down river to the sawmills and bringing freight up river for the logging camps.

Nine years later, 1892, Sam Van Sant was elected governor of the state of Minnesota. He served two terms from 1892 to 1896.

**Chippewa River Log Boom**

In the 1860's the logging companies were logging along the Chippewa River in western Wisconsin. They floated the logs down the Chippewa River to the boom site they had at Beef Slough, just above Alma, Wisconsin. Here the logs were sorted out and made up into rafts for the different sawmills down the river. To divert the logs when they came down the Chippewa River into the Beef Slough boom site, they installed a log boom across the Chippewa River about a half mile above the mouth of the Chippewa River where it entered the Mississippi River. At this time in history, the Chippewa River was much deeper than it is now. Soil erosion along the banks of the Chippewa hadn't started yet. Paddlewheel steamboats (the smaller ones) could go all the way up the Chippewa River during high water.

That diverting log boom that the loggers had across the river had to be moved when a paddlewheel steamboat wanted to pass. They had built it with several long 2 x 12 planks (rudders) that they attached to the log boom on the down stream side–extending down from the boom at about a 180 degree angle from the boom. They attached a cable to these planks (or rudders) so that the angle could be adjusted to keep the log boom in a closed position. The planks were at a 200 degree angle to the boom, and the river current would hold the log boom in a closed position since the boom was anchored on the north shore of the river. Then when a paddlewheel steamboat wanted to pass, the cable would be pulled so the angle of the rudder

*Str. "Golden Eagle" built in 1876 for Keokuk Northern Company. Courtesy Winona County Historical Society.*

(planks) was changed to about a 150 degree angle, and the current in the river would swing the log boom open, and the paddlewheel steamboat would pass. Then the angle of the rudders (planks) would be changed back to 200 degrees, and the current would swing the log boom back in place.

### River Pilots "Ash Pan School"
### at Albany, Illinois

When Sam Van Sant of LeClaire, Iowa, started moving the log rafts with paddlewheel steamboats, it was just natural that Steve Hanks of Albany, Illinois, with his knowledge of log rafting and the upper Mississippi River, ended up as a paddlewheel steamboat pilot moving log rafts down the Mississippi River. He was looked upon as the most experienced upper Mississippi River pilot.

In January, February, and March, when the upper Mississippi River was frozen, young pilots and cub pilots would come to Albany, Illinois, and stay for 2 to 4 weeks meeting with Captain Steve Hanks. Every morning except Sunday, they would meet at the General Store, sit around the pot belly stove, and talk about navigation problems on the upper Mississippi River–how to steer difficult bends and crossings–of which there were many. Captain Steve Hanks would use a long flat pan with wood ash spread out on it.

With a stick, he would draw a section of the river to illustrate what they were discussing. This is how "Ash Pan School" got its name. Captain Steve Hanks was a cousin of President Abraham Lincoln.

*Steve Hanks, farmer from Albany, Ill. took the first raft of logs down the Mississippi River.*
*Courtesy Winona County Historical Society.*

*Paddlewheel steamboat "Flying Eagle" excursion boat with it's excursion barge along side getting ready to leave on a cruise. Courtesy Winona County Historical Society.*

*Paddlewheel steamboat "Jacob Richtman" on an excursion cruise.*
*Courtesy Winona County Historical Society*

*Paddlewheel steamboat "Pilgrim" backing away from the bank to take the passsengers on an excursion cruise.*
*Courtesy Winona County Historical Society.*

*Paddlewheel excursion steamboat "Sunshine" on an excursion cruise.*
*Courtesy Winona County Historical Society.*

## Chapter Six
# *Upper Mississippi River Paddlewheel Steamboats 1823 to 1940*

T he first paddlewheel steamboat to make a run from St. Louis, Missouri, to St. Paul, Minnesota, was The "Virginia" in 1823. It was piloted by Captain Crawford. The purpose of the trip was to bring supplies to the troops at Fort Anthony, later named Fort Snelling, located just up the River from St. Paul where the Minnesota River enters the Mississippi.

John S. McCune and James E. Yeatman formed the first regular scheduled paddlewheel steamboat service on the upper Mississippi River in 1842–The St. Louis and Keokuk Packet Line. By 1865, they were operating twelve paddlewheel steamboats on the upper

Mississippi River.

In 1857, a group of paddlewheel steamboat owner captains in St. Louis, Missouri, joined together and formed the Northern Line Packet Company. By 1869, the Northern Line was operating twenty paddlewheel steamboats on the upper Mississippi River between St. Louis, Missouri, and St. Paul, Minnesota.

The Northern Company proved to be a strong competitor for the St. Louis and Keokuk Packet Line, and in 1871, the two companies merged. The new company was known as the Keokuk Northern Line. John S. McCune from the St. Louis and Keokuk Packet Line was selected President of the new Keokuk Northern

*Str. "Lucy Bertram" 1863-1876, wood hull, built at Madison, Ind. for
St. Louis and Keokuk Packet Co., 242 x 40 x 5.5, dismantled in 1876.
Courtesy Murphy Library, U. W-LaCrosse.*

*Str. "Tom Jasper" 1867-1878, side-wheel, wood hull, built at Madison, Ind. for Quincy and St. Paul Packet Co. 265 x 41 x 6.5, steam engines 27 inches diameter, 7 boilers. It was sold to Northwestern Union Line in 1876. They lengthened the hull 30 feet. After using the boat just 2 years on the upper Mississippi River, tied it off, and dismantled it in 1878. Courtesy Murphy Library, U. W.-LaCrosse.*

*Str. "Minneapolis" 1869-1870 side-heel, wood hull, built in Pittsburgh, Pa. 650 tons, 233 x 36 x 5.8, steam engines 30 inches in diameter with a 7 foot stroke, 4 boilers. It operated only two seasons. They dismantled it in the late fall of 1870. Courtesy Winona County Historical Society.*

*Str. "Key City" 1857-1869, side-wheel, wood hull, built in Cincinnati, Ohio for Minnesota Packet Co., 230 x 35 x 5.6, 560 tons.*
*On Oct. 4, 1857, it had a collision with the Str. "Ben Coursin" in a bend in the river by Dakota, Minn.*
*Both boats were salvaged and repaired. Courtesy Murphy Library, U. W.-LaCrosse.*

*Str. "Dubuque" 1867-1879, wood hull, built at Pittsburgh, Pa. for Northern Line Packet Co.*
*230 x 36 x 5.5, steam engines 20 inches in diameter with a 7 foot stroke.*
*On March 4, 1879, it burned to the waterline and sank in Alton Slough.*
*Courtesy Winona County Historical Society.*

Company. Business went real well for the new company until 1874. John S. McCune died. After his death, there was a lot of dissension between the stockholders. The end result was, six years later, Keokuk and Northern Packet Company went out of business in 1881.

That same year (1881), the St. Louis and St. Paul Packet Company was formed. It operated until 1889 when it sold out to the Diamond Jo Line. During this same period, there were other smaller river paddlewheel steamboat companies started on the upper Mississippi River. In 1847, Captain M. W. Ludwick bought the paddlewheel steamboat "Dr. Franklin". He called his company Minnesota Packet Company. He began making runs between Galena, Illinois, and St. Paul, Minnesota.

Ten years later, 1857, some investors in Dubuque, Iowa, had two paddlewheel steamboats built and started making runs between Dubuque, Iowa, and St. Paul, Minnesota. After just a couple years of operation, they merged with Captain Ludwick's company.

*Capt. William F. Davidson, owner of the Northwestern-Union Packet Line of LaCrosse, Wisc., at one time, had 30 paddlewheel steamboats working on the upper Mississippi River. Courtesy Murphy Library, U. W.-LaCrosse.*

In 1860, Captain William F. Davidson started the LaCrosse and St. Paul Packet Company. Through good business management and financial help from the LaCrosse and Milwaukee Railroad, he obtained control of Captain Ludwick's company and formed the Northwestern-Union Packet Line in 1866. Captain Davidson was now operating thirty paddlewheel steamboats. He had his own shipyard. But with the expansion of the railroads into the Wisconsin and Minnesota Territories served by the Northwestern-Union Packet Line, river traffic slowly declined. By 1873, the Northwestern-Union Packet Line was bankrupt.

At St. Paul, Minnesota, in the year 1855, there were 1058 paddlewheel steamboat arrivals. In 1874, just 16 years later, there were only 218 paddlewheel steamboats arrivals at St. Paul.

The last paddlewheel steamboat packet company to operate between St. Louis, Missouri, and St. Paul, Minnesota, was Captain Joseph Reynold's Diamond Jo Line with its headquarters at Dubuque, Iowa. Captain Jo started with just one paddlewheel steamboat in 1867. In 1889, Captain Jo took over all the assets of the St. Louis and St. Paul Packet Company. The Diamond Jo Line now was operating five paddlewheel steamboats between St. Louis, Missouri, and St. Paul, Minnesota. Most of the income (about 75%) now was from the passenger trade. Railroads had taken over the freight and mail business. By 1911,

*Str. "City of St. Paul", wood hull, 1866-?, built at LaCrosse, Wisc. for LaCrosse and St. Paul Packet Co.,
220 x 36 x 6, steam engines 21 inches in diameter with a 7 foot stroke, 3 boilers.
The machinery came from Str. "Moses McLillian".
Courtesy Winona County Historical Society.*

*Padlewheel steamboat "Dubuque". The hull and steam engines were salvaged fron the tornado damaged "Pittsburgh", 265.6 feet long with a beam of 50.7 feet. Steam engines 21 inches in diameter with a 7 foot stroke working 28 foot buckets. Converted into a day excursion boat in 1919 and named the "Capitol". Courtesy Winona County Historical Society.*

*Paddlewheel steamboat "J. S. Deluxe" 1919-1939, side paddlewheel, wood hull, rebuilt from the paddlewheel steamboat "Quincy", 265 x 42 x 7, steam engines 22 inches in diameter with 8 foot stroke. Courtesy Winona County Historical Society.*

*Paddlewheel steamboat "J. S." 1901-1910, wood hull, stern-wheel, built at Jefferson, Indiana for Streckfus Line.*
*This was the first paddlewheel steamboat disigned and built just for day excursion use.*
*175 x 33 x 5.5, steam engines 16 inches in diameter with a 6 foot stroke, 2 boilers.*
*It burned and sank by Bad Axe Island just below Genoa, Wisconsin in 1910.*
*Courtesy Winona County Historical Society.*

*Str. "Alex Mitchell", 1870-1881, sidewheel, wood hull, built in Paducah, Ky., completed in LaCrosse, Wisc. for Northwestern Union Packet Line. 241 x 37.5 x 5.5, steam engines 22 inches in diameter with an 8 foot stroke, 4 boilers. Machinery came from the Str. "St. Patrick". Alex Mitchell was president of the Milwaukee and St. Paul Railroad that had a working arrangement with Northwestern Union Packet. The boat was dismantled at LaCrosse, Wisc. in 1881. Courtesy Murphy Library, U. W.-LaCrosse.*

*Str. "Belle of LaCrosse" 1870-1882, side-wheel, wood hull, built at Paducah, Ky., completed at St. Louis, Mo. 232 x 37.8 x 5.5, steam engines 20 inches in diameter with a 7 foot stroke. Engines and machinery were salvaged from Str. "Itasca". Str. "Belle of LaCrosse" was destroyed by fire at St. Louis, Mo. July 12, 1882. Courtesy Murphy Library, U. W. - LaCrosse*

*Str. "St. Paul" 1883-1917, wood hull, side-wheel, built at Dubuque, Iowa for St. Louis and St. Paul Packet Co., 300 x 37.4 x 6.4, steam engines 21 inches in diameter with a 7 foot stroke. Paddlewheels were 26 ft. in diameter working 14 ft. buckets, 4 boilers. In 1889, it was sold to Diamond Jo Line, rebuilt at Dubuque in 1892 and again in 1903. It was sold to Streckfus Line in 1911, rebuilt into a day excursion boat in 1917 and renamed, "Excursion Queen St. Paul". Courtesy Winona County Historical Society.*

*Str. "Quincy" 1896-1919, wood hull, side-wheel, built at Dubuque, Iowa for Diamond Jo Line, 265 x 42 x 7, steam engines 22 inches in diameter with an 8 foot stroke. Hull and cabin came from the Str. "Gem City", steam engines from the Str. "Alex Mitchell". On July 11, 1906, it hit a snag and sank near Trempealeau, Wisc. It was raised and later sold to Streckfus Line, rebuilt into a day excursion boat and named the Str. "J.S. Deluxe". Courtesy Winona County Historical Society.*

*Str. "Sidney", 1880-1938, wood hull, stern-wheel, built at Murraysville, W. Va., 221 x 35.5 x 5.5, steam engines 17 inches in diameter with a 5.5 foot stroke, 3 boilers. In 1921, Streckfus Line completely rebuilt and converted the boat to a day excursion boat named the Str. "Washington". In 1938, it was dismantled. Courtesy Winona County Historical Society.*

*Paddlewheel steamboat "Washington" 1921-1938, wood hull, stern-wheel. This is the "Sidney" converted to a day excursion boat. 221 x 35.5 x 5.5, steam engines 17 inches in diameter with 5.5 foot stroke, 3 boilers.*
*Courtesy Winona County Historical Society*

*Paddlewheel steamboat "Saint Paul" 1883-1917, wood hull, side-wheel, built at Dubuque, Iowa.*
*300 x 37.4 x 6.4, steam engines 21 inch, 7 foot stroke.*
*Courtesy Winona County Historical Society.*

*Str. "Excursion Queen St. Paul", 1917-1939, wood hull, side-wheel, rebuilt from the Str. "St. Paul" by Streckfus Line and used as a day excursion boat, 300 x 37.4 x 6.4. In 1939, Streckfus Line remodeled it and changed the name to the "Senator" and put it to work on the Ohio River.*
*Courtesy Murphy Library, U. W.-LaCrosse.*

STRECKFUS EXCURSION STEAMER "SENATOR"
On the Ohio River

*Str. "Senator", 1939-1953, wood hull, side-wheel, 300 x 37.4 x 6.4, rebuilt from the Str. "Excursion Queen St. Paul".
In 1942, U. S. Coast Guard took it over and used it as a training vesseló dismantled in 1953.
Courtesy Murphy Library, U. W.-LaCrosse.*

*Capt. Joe Reynolds, owner of the Diamond Jo Line, the last packet boat company on the upper Mississippi River. Courtesy Winona County Historical Society.*

Diamond Jo Line was running only four boats: the "Quincy", "Dubuque", "St. Paul" and "Sidney". That same year, 1911, Captain Jo sold out to Streckfus Line in St. Louis, Missouri, which was already running paddlewheel steamboats in the river excursion business. By 1919, the Streckfus Line had converted all the paddlewheel steamboats they acquired from Captain Jo into excursion boats with large dance floors. The Streckfus Line kept some of the excursion boats all summer at a major river city. Others they would "tramp" up and down the Mississippi River stopping for a day or two at various smaller river towns.

The paddlewheel steamboat, "St. Paul", was built for St. Louis and St. Paul Packet Co. at the Dubuque Boat and Boiler Works in 1883. After

*Str. "J. S. Deluxe". 1919-1939, side-wheel, wood hull, rebuilt from the Str. "Quincy", 265 x 42 x 7, steam engines 22 inches in diameter with an 8 foot stroke. It was dismantled in 1939. This was the last side-wheel steamboat to operate on the upper Mississippi River. Courtesy Winona County Historical Society.*

*Str. "Pittsburgh", 1876-1896, wood hull, stern-wheel, built at Cincinnati, Ohio, 250 x 39 x 5.8, steam engines 21 inches in diameter with a 7 foot stroke working 28 foot buckets. In May, 1896, it was destroyed by a tornado at St. Louis, Mo. The hull and steam engines were salvaged and Diamond Jo Line used them to build the Str. "Dubuque". In 1919, Streckfus Line converted it to a day excursion boat and named it the Str. "Capitol". Courtesy Murphy Library, U. W.-LaCrosse.*

*This is the salvaged remains of the Str. "Pittsburgh" after it was destroyed by a tornado near St. Louis, Mo. in May, 1896. Diamond Jo Line bought it and used it to build the Str. "Dubuque". Courtesy Murphy Library, U. W.-LaCrosse.*

*Str. "Capitol", 1920-1945, stern-wheel, 265.6 feet long with a beam of 50.7 feet. This was the Str. "Dubuque" that Streckfus Line bought from Diamond Jo Line and remodeled into a day excursion boat in 1920. It was dismantled in 1945 at St. Louis, Mo. Courtesy Winona County Historical Society.*

*Str. "Cincinnati", 1924-1932, side-wheel, steel hull, 285 x 45.6 x 7.3, steam engines 22 inches and 40 inches in diameter with a 9 foot stroke, paddlewheels 30 feet in diameter working 16 foot buckets. In 1932, it was sold to Streckfus Steamers, Inc. rebuilt from the hull up as a day excursion boat, and renamed "President". Courtesy Murphy Library, U. W.-LaCrosse.*

*Cabin deck view of the paddlewheel steamboat "Cincinnati".*
*Courtesy Winona County Historical Society.*

*Str. "President" in construction stage at St. Louis, Missouri Levee. Courtesy Winona County Historical Society.*

*Str. "President", 1933, steel hull, side-wheel engines, machinery and hull came from the Str. "Cincinnati", 285 x 45.6 x 7.3, steam engines 22 inches in diameter with a 9 foot stroke, paddlewheels 30 feet in diameter working 16 foot buckets. Converted from steam paddlewheel to diesel prop in 1974 and remodeled into a casino boat in 1990. It is operating out of Davenport, Iowa. Courtesy Winona County Historical Society.*

*Paddlewheel steamboat "President" leaving lock 7 just above La Crosse, Wisconsin.*
*Courtesy Winona County Historical Society.*

Streckfus converted it in 1917, they changed its name to the "Excursion Queen St. Paul". It made excursion runs out of St. Louis, Missouri, every summer from 1917 to 1939. In 1939, Streckfus Line had it refitted and renamed the "Senator" and used it on the Ohio River. Then the U. S. Coast Guard took it over and used it as a training vessel during W.W. II. The "Senator" was dismantled in 1953.

*Str. "Albotross", side-wheel, steel hull, built at Dubuque, Iowa, 1907. 305 x 90, could carry 16 box cars at a time, steam engines 22 inches in diameter with a 10 foot stroke. Sold to Streckfus Steamers, Inc. in 1938.*
*Courtesy Winona County Historical Society.*

*Str. "Admiral", rebuilt and lengthened from the Str. "Albotross" in 1938, side-wheel, steel hull, 374 x 92, steam engines 26 inches in diameter with a 10 foot stroke, 1500 HP, 4400 passengers. In 1974, steam engines and paddlewheels were removed, and it was converted to diesel and prop drive. It was tied off at St. Louis, Mo. in 1979 and remodeled into a permanently moored entertainment center. Courtesy Winona County Historical Society.*

The paddlewheel steamboat, "Quincy" also was converted in 1919 by Streckfus Line and renamed "J.S. Deluxe". J.S. were John Streckfus' initials. They kept it in St. Louis also with the "Excursion Queen St. Paul". The "J.S. Deluxe" was used in the excursion boat business up to 1939 when it was dismantled.

In 1896, a tornado went through the St. Louis area, and it demolished the paddlewheel steamboat,

*Paddlewheel steamboat "Admiral" a day excursion boat. Courtesy Winona County Historical Society.*

"Pittsburgh". The hull and steam engines were salvaged. Diamond Jo Line had it rebuilt and outfitted as the "Dubuque". Diamond Jo Line sold the "Dubuque" to the Streckfus Line in 1911. In 1919, the Streckfus Line had the Dubuque shipyard take the hull and steam engines of the old "Dubuque" and rebuild it as an excursion boat which they named, "Capitol". Streckfus used it to "tramp" up and down the Mississippi River stopping a day or two at the river towns. The "Capitol" was dismantled at St. Louis in 1945.

In 1932, the Streckfus Line bought the paddlewheel steamboat, "Cincinnati" that was built for the Ohio River Packet Company in 1924-25. Streckfus converted it into a day excursion boat and named it "President". The "President" made runs out of St. Louis, Missouri, in the summer and out of New Orleans, Louisiana, in the winter. Then in 1938, Streckfus Line bought the paddlewheel steamboat railroad ferry boat, "Albatross" that Vicksburg Railroad had built in 1907. Streckfus Line had it converted into a modern streamline-looking day excursion boat and renamed it the "Admiral". It entered the excursion boat business at St. Louis in 1940.

From then on, the paddlewheel steamboat, "President" stayed in New Orleans year round. The "Admiral" was the first excursion boat to have air conditioning. In 1974, the steam engines and paddlewheels were removed from both the "Admiral" and the "President". Diesel engines and props were installed on both boats. The "Admiral" was taken out of service in 1979 because it could not pass Coast Guard hull inspection. It is now permanently moored on the St. Louis River Front Levee. The "President" was sold to Gateway Clipper Fleet. It was converted into a river casino boat in 1990. It started river boat gambling operation out of Davenport, Iowa, in 1991.

*Paddlewheel steamboat "Gordon Green" an overnight excursion boat.*
*The "Gordon Green" was used in the movie "Gone With The Wind".*
*Courtesy Winona County Historical Society.*

*Paddlewheel steamboat "Chris Green", overnight excursion boat.*
*Courtesy Winona County Historical Society.*

*Dance floor on Streckfus Line day excursion paddlewheel steamboat, "Senator".*
*Courtesy Murphy Library, U. W.-LaCrosse.*

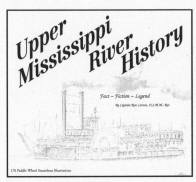

# Chapter Seven
# *Today's Paddlewheel Steamboats*

Str. "Delta Queen", Str. "Mississippi Queen", Str. "Belle of Louisville",
Str. "Julia Belle Swain", Str. "Natchez", Str. "American Queen"

### Paddlewheel Steamboat
### "Delta Queen"

The riveted steel hull for the paddlewheel steamboat, "Delta Queen", was fabricated in Scotland at the same shipyard that built the "Queen Mary". It was shipped in sections to San Francisco, California, where it was assembled. The upper decks and cabins were constructed at Stockton, California, on the Sacramento River. In 1926, when it was completed, she joined the "Delta King" in overnight service between Sacramento and San Francisco, California, on the Sacramento River. In

World War II, the U. S. Government took both boats over and used them as ferry boats in San Francisco Bay. Shortly after the war, 1947, the U. S. Government sold the paddlewheel steamboats as government surplus equipment. Captain Tom Green, owner of Green Line Steamers of Cincinnati, Ohio, bought the paddlewheel steamboat, "Delta Queen". He had it towed down through to Panama Canal and up to New Orleans. Then under its own power, he had Captain Way bring her up the Mississippi River into the Ohio River up to Dravo's shipyard at Pittsburgh, Pennsylvania–a 5,000 mile sea, canal, and river journey. After extensive refit and alterations, the paddle-

*Str. "Delta Queen", 1926, steel hull stern-wheel, built at Stockton, Calif., 285 x 58.2 x 9, steam engines, cross compound with a 26 and 52.5 inch diameter cylinders with a 10 foot stroke, 2 boilers. Courtesy Winona Historical Society.*

*Str. "Mississippi Queen", 1976, steel hull, stern-wheel, built by Jeffboat at Jeffersonville, Ind., 379 x 68 x 12, steam engines, reciprocating tandem compound, high pressure cylinder, 16 inches in diameter, low pressure cylinder, 32 inches in diameter with a 10 foot stroke, 2 boilers. Paddlewheel 22.9 feet in diameter working 36 foot buckets.*
*Courtesy Winona County Historical Society.*

EXCURSION STEAMER

"AVALON"

*Str. "Avalon"-"Idlewild", stern-wheel, steel hull, built at Pittsburgh, Pa. in 1914. 157 x 36 x 5, steam engines 16 inches in diameter with 6.5 foot stroke, 3 boilers, paddlewheel 19 feet in diameter working 24 foot buckets. It came out in 1914 as the Str. "Idlewild", renamed the "Avalon" in 1948. It was bought by Jefferson County, Ky. in 1962 and renamed the "Belle of Louisville". Courtesy Winona County Historical Society.*

*Str. "Idlewild", 1914, steel hull, stern-wheel, built at Pittsburgh, Pa. 157 x 36 x 5, steam engines 16 inches in diameter with a 6.5 foot stroke, 3 boilers. It was renamed Str. "Avalon" in 1948, bought by Jefferson Co., Ky. in 1962 and named Str. "Belle of Louisville". Courtesy Winona County Historical Society.*

wheel steamboat, "Delta Queen", entered the river cruise excursion service on the Ohio and Mississippi Rivers in June of 1948. This included two or three trips on the upper Mississippi River to St. Paul, Minnesota, each year. In 1991, the paddlewheel steamboat, "Delta Queen", was laid up in dry dock in New Orleans at Arvondale shipyard. She received a new welded steel hull. The paddlewheel steamboat,

"Delta Queen", has accommodations for one hundred and ninety-two passengers. Her hull is 285 feet in length, including the paddlewheel with a beam of 59 feet. From the water line to the top of her stack is 55 feet. Her steam engines produce 1000 horsepower.

## Paddlewheel Steamboat
## "Mississippi Queen"

In 1973, Green Line Steamers was bought out by the Delta Queen Steamboat Company. That fall, the Delta Queen Steamboat Company had the shipyard, Jeffboat, at Jeffersonville, Indiana, on the Ohio River build the paddlewheel steamboat, "Mississippi Queen" at a cost of 27 million dollars. She entered regular river cruise service on the Mississippi and Ohio Rivers in 1977. The paddlewheel steamboat, "Mississippi Queen", is 382 feet in overall length with a beam of 68 feet. The two tandem compound condensing steam engines develop 2000 horsepower and turn a 36 foot wide, 22 foot diameter paddlewheel. The steamboilers are oil fired, burning #6 bunker C oil–about 250 gallons per hour. She has overnight accommodations for 471 passengers and carries a crew of 140. From the water line to the top of her stacks when they are fully extended is 80 feet.

## Paddlewheel Steamboat
## "Belle of Louisville"

About the same time after World War II that the paddlewheel steamboat, "Delta Queen" started cruising on the Mississippi River, the paddlewheel steamboat "Avalon" began day excursion cruises tramping on the upper Mississippi River. This paddlewheel steamboat was built in 1914, originally named "Idlewild". She was used as a river packet boat and ferry for a while. After two or three different companies were unsuccessful in their attempts to operate the "Idlewild" at a profit, in 1947, Mr. J. Herod Gorsage bought the "Idlewild". Then to honor the deathbed wish of her Master, Captain Ben Winters, Mr. Gorsage renamed it the "Avalon" and sold it in 1949 to the Steamer Avalon Corporation. The first few years the "Avalon" was successful in its day excursion and evening dance cruises, stopping for a day or two "tramping" up and down the Mississippi River, and its tributaries. But in 1962, the Steamer Avalon Corporation went out of business, and the Federal Marshall sold the paddlewheel steamboat, "Avalon", to pay its creditors. It was bought by Jefferson County of Kentucky. They had it refitted and renamed it the "Belle of Louisville". The paddlewheel steamboat, "Belle of Louisville" still operates out of the port of Louisville, Kentucky, making day excursions and dance cruises all summer long.

*Str. "Belle of Louisville", stern-wheel, steel hull. In 1962, it was rebuilt from the Str. "Idlewild". 157 x 36 x 5, steam engines 16 inches in diameter with a 6.5 foot stroke, 3 boilers, paddlewheel 19 feet in diameter working 24 foot buckets. Oldest Mississippi River paddlewheel steamboat in existence. Courtesy Belle of Louisville Operating Board.*

**Paddlewheel Steamboat**
**"Julia Belle Swain"**

The steamboat, "Julia Belle Swain" operates on the upper Mississippi River making overnight trips from LeClaire, Iowa, to Battle Mountain Resort on the river backwater near Galena, Illinois. It is a steel hull boat built at Dubuque, Iowa, in 1971. Overall dimensions are 149 X 27, steam engines 12 inches in diameter with a 5 foot stroke.

**Paddlewheel Steamboat**
**"Natchez"**

There is another paddlewheel steamboat that is operating on the Mississippi River. But it has never been on the upper Mississippi. It is the paddlewheel steamboat, "Natchez", out of the port of New Orleans, Louisiana. The "Natchez" runs daily sightseeing cruises, luncheon and dinner cruises and evening dance cruises.

*Str. "Julia Belle Swain", paddlewheel steamboat that made overnight trips between LeClaire, Iowa, and Battle Mountain Resort on the upper Mississippi River. Courtesy Winona County Historical Society.*

The paddlewheel steamboat, "Natchez", was constructed in 1975 for the New Orleans Steamboat Company. The "Natchez" is 285 feet in length overall with a beam of 50 feet. It is powered by tandem compound condensing steam engines rated at 1500 horsepower. These steam engines came from the old paddlewheel steamboat, "Clairton". The paddlewheel steamboat, "Natchez" is elegantly furnished and fully air conditioned throughout the steamboat.

### Paddlewheel Steamboat
### "American Queen"

The Delta Queen Steamboat Company named their third paddlewheel steamboat "American Queen". She was built at a cost of 65 million dollars. She has six decks, 418 feet long, with a beam of 89 feet. From the water line to the top of the twin fancy fluted stacks, when raised, is 105 feet.

*Str, "American Queen". 1994-1995, steel hull, stern-wheel, 418 x 89, high pressure steam engines from the U.S. Army Corps of Engineers dredge "Kennedy". With backup twin diesel engines. Courtesy Delta Queen Steamboat Company.*

*New Orleans Steamboat Company excursion boat, the paddlewheel str., "Natchez". Courtesy Winona County Historical Society.*

The rebuilt steam engines came out of the U.S. Army Corps of Engineers dredge "Kennedy". The steam engines are Nordberg compound, horizontal, reciprocating engines. They are rated at 700 horsepower each. The "American Queen" also has two Aquamaster-Rauma US911/2250 1000hp diesel engines to assist the steam engines when extra power is needed. These diesel engines also serve as stern thrusters when docking and going through locks. The "American Queen" entered regular weekly river cruises in the summer of 1995. She has accommodations for 420 passengers and a crew of 138.

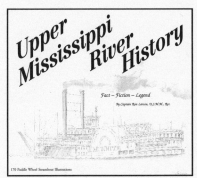

## Chapter Eight
# *Wing Dams on the Upper Mississippi River*

Purpose of Wing Dams and How They Were Built

To improve navigation on the upper Mississippi River from St. Louis, Missouri, to St. Paul, Minnesota, Congress passed, in 1907, legislation so the U. S. Army of Engineers could go ahead with their plans to develop the upper Mississippi River for six foot draft vessels by placing thousands of rock and brush wing dams.

The purpose of the wing dams was to confine the river to a narrow channel during low water periods so the paddlewheel steamboats could still navigate on the upper Mississippi River. To build these wing dams, which were piles of rock extending out from the shore sometimes five to six hundred feet, the Army Engineers had a crew first cut a lot of brush and make it into a raft. This raft was anchored over the site where they wanted a wing dam to be built. Then they brought in a barge loaded with stone quarried out of a bluff near by. They tied the rock barge off just below the raft of brush. Then a crew of men threw the stone on the brush raft until the brush raft sank to the bottom of the river. By the time that raft sunk, the brush and raft crew had another raft ready to float into place where the other had sunk. They kept repeating this procedure until they built up the wing dam to the required height. The wing dams worked very well. Not only did they help extend navigation during low

*A close look at a wing dam before the lock and dams were built and raised the water lever over them.*
*Courtesy Winona County Historical Society.*

*A U.S. Army Corps of Engineers building a wing dam with brush and rock.*
*Courtesy Winona County Historical Society.*

*This is a good bird's eye view of the upper Mississippi River before the lock and dam system was built showing the wing dams.*
*Courtesy Winona County Historical Society.*

water periods, they also stabilized the main channel, and islands didn't appear and disappear like they did before.

When they put in the lock and dam system which we have now, the water level was raised above the stone wing dams. They are still there just a few inches below the surface waiting for a boater who is unfamiliar with the upper Mississippi River to go by, and it will take a chunk out of the bottom of his boat.

*Double incline rail to bring rock for wing dams down from the quarry up on the top of the bluff. Courtesy Winona County Historical Society.*

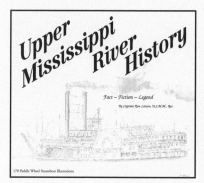

## Chapter Nine
# *Lock and Dams on the Upper Mississippi River*

The Changes Made by Army Engineers, How a Double Lockage is Done.

Congress decided that there would be a good economic savings for the Upper Midwest states if bulk freight, such as coal, grain, steel, petroleum, and chemicals could be transported on the upper Mississippi River in nine-foot draft barges. So they passed legislation in 1930 which asked the U. S. Army Engineers to design and build a lock and dam system to maintain a main channel on the upper Mississippi River from St. Louis, Missouri, to Minneapolis, Minnesota, for nine-foot draft vessels.

It took the Army Engineers about two years to complete the mapping to determine how many locks and dams would have to be built. At Minneapolis,

Minnesota, the Ford Power Lock and Dam was already in place. This the Army Engineers designated as Lock and Dam Number One. Also the Power Lock and Dam at Keokuk, Iowa, which was built in 1913 was in place. This was named Lock and Dam Number Nineteen. By 1932, all the planning was completed, and construction was started on twenty-four lock and dams from Hastings, Minnesota, to Alton, Illinois. The Army Engineers did not give these lock and dams names. They gave them numbers–although the local citizens called them by the name of the town they were built close to, such as the Hastings Lock and Dam, which the Army Engineers named Number Two,

*Bird's eye view of Lock and Dam Number 4 at Alma, Wisc.*
*Courtesy Winona County Historical Society.*

*U.S. Army Corps of Engineers paddlewheel steamboat, "Muscatine" locking through with a rock barge shortly after the lock was built.*
*Courtesy Winona County Historical Society.*

or the Alma Lock and Dam, which the Army Engineers named Lock and Dam Number Four.

The lock and dam at Alma, Wisconsin: Lock and Dam Number Four was the first site to get started. The others followed shortly after, except Lock and Dam Number Twenty-Three at Louisiana, Missouri, and Lock and Dam Number Five A located just three miles above Winona, Minnesota. The Army Engineers thought that maybe if they built Lock and Dam Twenty-Four to provide a lift a fifteen feet instead of the planned ten feet, and with some extra dredging and diking, they could eliminate Lock and Dam Twenty-Three which was originally included in their plans. This proved to be right. So Lock and Dam Twenty-Three never was built.

As work progressed with construction of Lock and Dam Six at Trempealeau, Wisconsin, about fifteen miles down river from Winona, Minnesota, the Army

*Lock and Dam Number 1 at Minneapolis, Minn. It has a 38 foot lift.*
*Courtesy Winona County Historical Society.*

Engineers realized they would raise the water level at Winona so high it would flood out a large part of the town of Winona, Minnesota. So they decided to add another lock and dam above Winona, Minnesota. Since all the locks were already assigned numbers, they gave the lock and dam above Winona, the number Five- A. This does make things confusing to some of the pleasure boaters who don't pay attention to their river charts or the Coast Guard Light List when they first start cruising on the Mississippi River. First they

*The Str. "Patrick J. Hurley" locking up at Lock #11 at Dubuque, Iowa.*
*Courtesy Winona County Historical Society.*

find out when calling the lock and dam on the marine radio by the name of the town it's by. They learn they should call it by the number given it by the Army Engineers. Then when they get to Lock and Dam Five-A, they are calling it Lock Six or Lock Five which ends up to be very comical radio communications at times.

Because Lock and Dam Five-A was added after Lock and Dam Five and Six were started, Lock Five and Six have only a lift of six feet each. This is the

*15 Barge tow locking down at one of the upper Mississippi River locks.*
*Courtesy U. S. Army Engineers.*

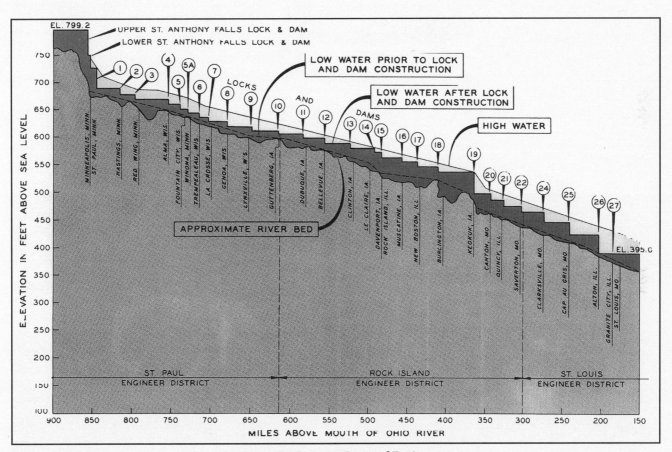

*Courtesy U. S. Army Corps of Engineers.*

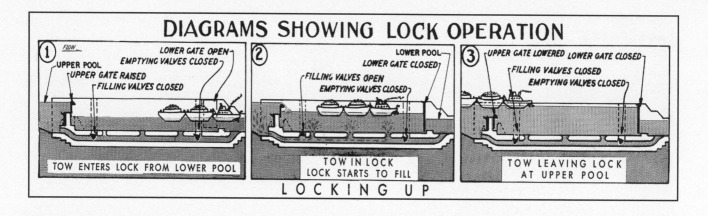

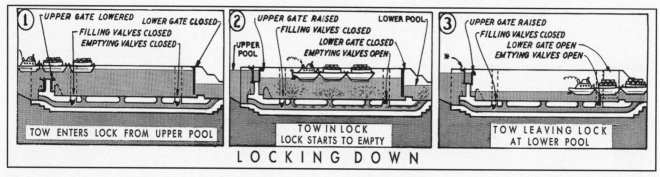

*Courtesy U. S. Army Corps of Engineers.*

smallest lift of all the locks on the upper Mississippi River. Lock Nineteen and Lock One have lifts of thirty-eight feet. Lock Twenty-Six has a lift of twenty-five feet. Locks Twenty-Five, Twenty-Four and Fifteen have lifts of fifteen feet each. The rest of the lock and dams of the first twenty-four built on the upper Mississippi River have a lift of about ten feet. By 1939, all the lock and dams on the upper Mississippi River were in operation.

*Upper and Lower St. Anthony Falls locks at Minneapolis, Minnesota.  Courtesy U. S. Army Engineers.*

When the lock and dams were first constructed, they all had one lock chamber with provisions to add an auxiliary lock chamber if the volume of commercial traffic justifies it.

The main lock chambers are one hundred and ten feet wide, six hundred feet long. They are large enough to take nine barges at a time. The Army Engineers constructed them so they can raise and lower the water in the lock chamber using a very economical system. They use gravity.

Any boat can use the lock. Towboats, when they buy their fuel, pay a fuel tax of nineteen cents a gallon, and some of this money goes to the Army Engineers to maintain and operate the lock and dams.

Lock One is smaller. It is only fifty-six feet wide by four hundred feet in length.

Only two of the first twenty-four lock and dams have had the auxiliary lock chamber added: Lock Fifteen at Rock Island, Illinois, and Lock Twenty-Six at Alton, Illinois.

After World War II, the Army Engineers added two more locks to the upper Mississippi River. First at East St. Louis, they constructed the Chain of Rocks Canal and Lock Twenty-Seven to bypass Sawyer's Bend, which was very rocky and had a very fast current. Lock Twenty-Seven has two lock chambers. The main chamber is twelve hundred feet long and one hundred and ten feet wide. It is large enough to take fifteen barges and the towboat all at once. The auxiliary lock chamber is six hundred feet long and one hundred and ten feet wide.

The other lock the Army Engineers constructed after World War II is actually twin locks, two locks in a row. They are located at Minneapolis, Minnesota. They lift the boats up over Saint Anthony Falls. These lock chambers, like Lock Number One are fifty-six feet wide and four hundred feet long. The lower lock has a lift of twenty-five feet. The upper lock has a lift of forty-nine feet.

When the Army Engineers were making a routine inspection in 1960 of Lock and Dam Twenty-Six at Alton, Illinois, they found there was need of some major rebuilding. The large volume of commercial barge traffic (both from the upper Mississippi and Illinois Rivers) passing through Lock Twenty-Six was causing, at times, delays of two to three days for the commercial tows. The Army Engineers recommended to Congress to authorize construction of a new lock and dam at Alton, Illinois, with two twelve hundred feet lock chambers. This would eliminate most of the lock delays. The cost would be very little more than the major repairs to Lock Twenty-Six, and the economical saving would be many times more than the cost.

Although there is still work to be done on the new lock and dam at the time of this writing, Lock and Dam Twenty-Six has been removed, and one of the

*Here we can see the close fit of a tow that is three barges wide in the lock chamber.*
*The tow is 105 feet wide and the lock chamber is 110 feet wide. Courtesy U. S. Army Engineers.*

*Str. "Alexander Mackenzie", 1939-1954, stern-wheel, steel hull, built at Point Pleasant, W.Va.  167 x 37.5 x 8.4,
steam engines 16 and 32 inches in diameter with a 10 foot stroke.  It was dismantled in 1954.  Here it is
locking up with its tow at Lock 19 at Keokuk, Iowa.  Courtesy Winona County Historical Society.*

lock chambers in the new dam is in use.  The Army Engineers named this new lock, Melvin Price.

Many years ago, Congress established the priority list for boats locking on Federal waters.  Government boats are first, then boats carrying U. S. Mail, then boats with passengers for hire, fourth is commercial towboats, and last pleasure boats.

On the upper Mississippi River, commercial towboats are allowed to make two lockages at the six hundred foot locks.  This means the largest number a

*Tow Boat "Alexander Mackenzie" taking the first 15 barge tow of coal up to St. Paul, Minnesota after the lock and dam system was completed on the Upper Mississippi River.*

barges a towboat will have is fifteen, unless it has empty barges in tow. Then sometimes, they will put empty barges along side the towboat. It is possible to see a tow of sixteen and sometimes seventeen barge tow on the upper Mississippi River.

One barge is thirty-five feet wide and two hundred feet long. A tow that is three barges wide and five barges long is one hundred and five feet wide and one thousand feet in length. Except for the locks at Minneapolis on the upper Mississippi River, locks are one hundred and ten feet wide. There is room for three barges wide with about two and one half feet clearance on each side. At the six hundred foot locks, a fifteen barge tow has to make two lockage to get all the barges and towboats through.

This requires a lot of skill and patience. First, the tow has to be worked into the lock. Then the first nine barges are tied off in the lock chamber and separated from the other six barges and towboat. The towboat backs the six barges out of the lock chamber. The lock gates are closed. Water in the lock chamber is either raised or lowered. Lock gates on the other end of the lock chamber are opened. The nine barges are moved out of the lock. This is done in one of two ways depending whether the tow is going up river or down. If the tow is going up river, there is a winch at the lock that is used to pull the first nine barges out of the lock chamber, and they are tied along the wall above the lock. If the tow is going down river, they use a differ-

ent system. After the water in the lock chamber is lowered, the lower lock chamber gates are opened. Then the operator of the lock opens the valves he uses to fill the lock chamber. But since the lower lock chamber gates are open, the water runs out of the lock chamber taking the nine barges with it. Then the mate and his deckhands riding on the nine barges catch pegs along the wall below the lock chamber with heavy lines and stop the nine barges and tie them off below the lock chamber.

After the first nine barges have been brought through the lock chamber, the gates are closed. The water in the chamber is either raised or lowered so that the other six barges of the tow, and the towboat can be brought into the lock chamber. When the towboat moves the six barges out of the lock chamber, they have to line them up with the first nine and cable them back together. Then the tow can leave the lock and continue on its way. A double lockage like this takes about an hour and a half to two hours.

After the first twenty-four lock and dams on the upper Mississippi River were completed, it wasn't until after World War II (1947) that a fifteen barge tow made a run all the way from St. Louis, Missouri, to St. Paul, Minnesota. It was a fifteen barge tow of coal pushed by the paddlewheel steamboat, the "Alexander Mackinzie", and piloted by Captain Walter Karnath of Winona, Minnesota.

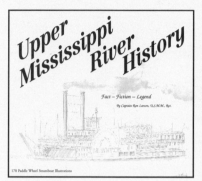

# Chapter Ten
# *Mississippi River Navigation Aids*

River Charts, Coast Guard Light List, Day Boards (Channel Markers), Buoys

G ood detailed charts have been prepared by Army Engineers survey crews of all navigable inland waterways. These charts can be purchased at most marinas and from the U. S. Army Corps of Engineers.

Another useful aid is the U. S. Coast Guard's Light List. This is a publication that lists all buoys that show a blinking light, dock lights, daymarks with mile boards, lock and dams, and bridge clearances.

On the Mississippi River, the U. S. Coast Guard has the responsibility of maintaining the buoys marking the main river channel. Red buoys are on the right as you go up the river. The red buoys are also shaped so

*Courtesy U.S. Army Corps of Engineers.*

*U.S. Coast Guard Light List. Courtesy U.S. Coast Guard.*

that they come to a point on the top. On the other side of the channel–the left side going up river–there will be green buoys (these used to be black). The green buoys are flat on top, like a tin can. The buoys are about ten feet in height, and weigh about five hundred pounds. The buoys are weighted and designed so they float straight up. When in the water only about a third of the buoy is above the surface, two-thirds of the buoy is below the surface. Then there is a heavy chain or cable that goes from the bottom of the buoy to a concrete anchor that holds that buoy on station. If you look closely at the buoys as you go by, you will see that the top of the buoy is constructed with two pieces of flat steel at right angles to each other and look like

*Coast Guard Buoy Tender "Wyaconda" going into the Ice Harbor at Dubuque, Iowa.*

fins on a bomb. The reason for this is these flat surfaces reflect a radar signal much better than the round surface. So the buoys will show up on the radar screen as a small dot.

Another navigation aid that the Coast Guard maintains is the flashing light dayboards that are usually located on shore, but sometimes on a piling out in the river.

This system got started on the lower Ohio River in 1860 by the River Pilots Association. They set up a beacon light system with kerosene lanterns with two white boards in an X nailed to a tree or a post along the shore to give the pilots a reference point to steer by.

The Coast Guard recognized the value of this guidance system, and in 1875, asked Congress to authorize a Federal Dayboard and Beacon system on our rivers.

The beacon lights were kerosene lanterns until 1960. Then they were changed over to battery operated flashing lights. In the 1980's, the Coast Guard mounted, on the dayboards, a small solar panel that recharges the batteries so they last for years.

After the Coast Guard had established the beacon

*Navigation Aid.*
*Captain Ron Larson Photo.*

light and dayboard system, they started adding mileage boards to them. By this time, the river pilots had given each dayboard a different name. These names, at the insistence of the river pilots, was officially accepted and added to the Coast Guard Light List Publication. The river pilots use these navigation dayboard names when they are talking to each other on the marine radio to fix their positions so they will know how soon they will be meeting each other.

Men that tended the dayboard kerosene beacon lanterns were hired by the Army Engineers. Each day they would start out in a rowboat, cleaning and filling a lantern as they floated down the river to the next dayboard. When they had finished their section of the river, their partner (this was sometimes their wife) would be waiting with a team and wagon to bring the lantern tender and rowboat back up to the starting point for the next day's run. After World War I, the wagons started to be replaced by trucks.

From Cairo, Illinois, which is mile zero on the upper Mississippi River to the head of navigation mile eight fifty-seven point six at Minneapolis, Minnesota, there are three hundred and fifty-nine beacon dayboards.

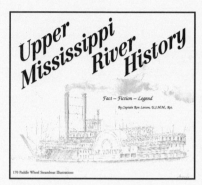

## Chapter Eleven
# *River Pilot Stories by Captain Ron*

Fact-Fiction-Legend

**"Grass-hopping" Over a Sandbar**

At times, a major shallow sandbar would block the main channel. The crew would attempt various maneuvers. First, they would temporarily off load freight and passengers on shore to lighten the paddlewheel steamboat. Then as a last resort, the deck crew would rig two large spars (they were like large power poles) setting them at a slight angle in the riverbed just ahead of the boat on each side of the bow, then with two lines (heavy rope) fasten to the bow up to pulleys at the top of the spars and back down to the bow through pulleys and over to the capstan. Then the pilot would signal for slow ahead. This would cause the bow to raise as though it were on crutches, and the boat would move ahead. This slow and laborious work would be repeated until the paddlewheel steamboat was clear of the sandbar.

**German Immigrants Stranded**

A paddlewheel steamboat (Name unknown) with about 25 German immigrant families on board ran aground on a sandbar, just above Island 65 on the upper Mississippi River, which is located about 4 or 5 miles above the city of Winona, Minnesota. It was

*Str. "Andy Johnson", 1866-1876, wood hull, side-wheel, built at Madison, Ind., steam engines 28.5 inches in diameter with a 7 foot stroke. On Dec. 13, 1876, it was cut down and destroyed by an ice floe at St. Louis, Mo. Courtesy Murphy Library, U.W.-LaCrosse.*

late in the fall when the river was low. To lighten the paddlewheel steamboat so it could pass over the sandbar, the German immigrants, with all their household goods and personal luggage, were put ashore on Island 65. This lightened the paddlewheel steamboat enough so the pilot was able to maneuver the boat over the sandbar. After they got over the sandbar, they just kept going up the river leaving the German immigrants stranded on Island 65 in freezing weather with a minimum of provisions.

**Mississippi River Clams (Pearl Bottom Clams)**

In the upper Mississippi River, there are many locations where there are clam beds with thousands of clams. These freshwater clams are edible. I can attest to that. I have eaten many of them. But except for the American Indian, they haven't caught on like the ocean clam or salt water oysters. Mr. Boepple, a German button maker, discovered he could make buttons from the Mississippi clam shell. So, in 1887, he immigrated to America and, in 1891, set up shop at Muscatine, Iowa, because he found a real good source of Mississippi clams in the back water sloughs there. He called his company, The Hawkeye Pearl Button Company.

As the pearl button business grew, some of Boepple's employees left and started their own button

*This is a commercial clammer using the Braille method.*

factories. By 1897, there were eleven button factories in Muscatine, Iowa. By now, almost every town on the upper Mississippi River from Muscatine, Iowa, to Lake Pepin, Minnesota, had a clam shell button factory. But most of the others just cut the round blanks out of the shells and shipped them by paddlewheel steamboat to the pearl button factories in Muscatine, Iowa. When the round button blanks arrived at the pearl button factories in Muscatine, Iowa, they were sliced into thin buttons, polished, and had the holes drilled into them.

Many farmers along the upper Mississippi River set themselves up with a clamming operation. All they

*Mr. Boepple.*
*Courtesy Winona County Historical Society.*

needed was a flatbottom boat, which they usually built themselves. They also needed a length of 3/4 inch pipe about 14 feet long to which were attached 3 foot lines at intervals of four inches. At the end of these lines was a wire crowfoot hook. When this was dragged over the clam bed, the clams would clamp onto the crowfoot hook and wouldn't let go. Usually after floating over a clam bed, 20 to 25 clams would end up clamped to the crowfoot hooks. The pipe rack was pulled up, and the clams pulled off. Then they would row the boat back up above the clam bed and repeat this process until the boat was full. This type of clamming was called the braille system. The boat load of

*Crow Foot Hook*

clams was brought ashore, and the clams were put into a big tub of boiling water. Immediately the clams would open, and all the clam meat was removed. The clam shells and meat were checked for slugs, river

*These round blanks cut from clam shells were shipped to the button factory where they were sliced, polished, and drilled so they could be used for buttons.*
*Courtesy Winona County Historical Society.*

pearls. The meat was used for hog and chicken feed, and the shells sold to a local shell dealer or shipped by paddlewheel steamboat to a button factory. The clam shells sold for about $40 a ton.

Clamming is still done on the upper Mississippi River. Now it is under Federal control, and the clammers have to be licensed by the Federal Government. Undersized clams have to be thrown back. Some of today's clammers use the old braille method, but more and more of the clammers use diving equipment. Now days, the meat from the clams goes into cat and dog food, and the shells are shipped to Japan. But they don't make buttons out of the shells. The Japanese place small pieces of the Mississippi clam

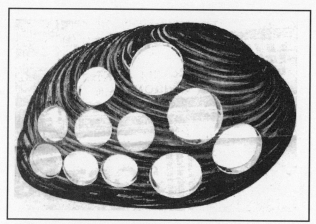

*Clam shell after blanks are cut out. Courtesy Winona County Historical Society.*

shell into a oyster, and the oyster makes a pearl from it. So the pearls you ladies have, got its beginning on the bottom of the Mississippi River.

Old clam shells with round holes cut in them can still be found along the banks of the upper Mississippi River where there used to be a button factory. One of these early clam shell button factories that is still making buttons is located in Lansing, Iowa. Of course, they make their buttons out of plastic now.

### Betsey Slough

This is how the section of the upper Mississippi channel below Fountain City, Wisconsin, got its name, "Betsey Slough". This happened in the late 1800's during the log rafting days. A log raft pilot that everybody on the river called "Pappy" and his crew of raftmen were taking a large raft of logs down the Mississippi River. Pappy's wife, Betsey, always went along to cook for the crew. Pappy would set up a tent for her in the middle of the log raft so she would be out of the way when they worked the 30-foot long sweeps (oars) to guide the log raft around the bends as they floated down the river.

When the log raft got to the bend below Fountain City, Wisconsin, it landed on the point on the upper end of the island and the log raft broke into two. The forward half went down the back channel chute, and the other half with Betsey went down the main channel through the slough. The two sections of the raft and most of the stray logs that broke loose met again down around the bend below the island. The raftmen put the two raft sections back together again and continued down the Mississippi to the sawmill. Soon after this happened, all the raftmen and river pilots heard the story about this log raft break up. Before long, they started calling the back channel "Pappy's Chute" and the main channel through the slough, "Betsey's Slough". The river pilots today still call it "Betsey's Slough".

*Log raft being guided down the upper Mississippi River by raftmen. Courtesy Murphy Library, U.W.-LaCrosse.*

### Cordova, Illinois

This is a river story about how the city of Cordova got its name. In the early paddlewheel steamboat days when they were burning cord wood in their boilers , there was a Scandinavian immigrant that had a wood-yard at this landing, selling cord wood to the paddle-wheel steamboats. Since he was new in America, he had learned to count to only ten in English. So when the captains would ask him how many cords of wood

*Str. "Lake Superior", 1870-1879, wood hull, side-wheel, built at Wheeling, W.Va.*
*240 x 39 x 6, steam engines 22.5 inches in diameter with a 7 foot stroke, paddlewheels 28 foot*
*in diameter working 12.5 foot buckets. On March 4, 1879, it burned and sank in Alton Slough.*
*Courtesy Murphy Library, U.W.-LaCrosse.*

he had loaded on their boat–if it was fourteen cords, he would answer, "Four cords ova ten". Soon the paddlewheel steamboat captains started calling this wood-yard landing cord ova landing. It's been known as Cordova ever since.

### "Tete du Morts Creek"

There is a creek in Iowa that enters the Mississippi River just across the river from Galena, Illinois. The early French fur traders gave it a French name. They called it "Tete du Morts". Translated, it means "heads of death".

Back before the white man was here, this was all American Indian territory. The land south of what is now the state of Minnesota was Sac territory. North was Sioux territory. A band of Sioux braves had made a raid on a Sac village. As they were making their way back north, they set up an ambush for the Sac warriors who were pursuing them here by this creek. The Sac warriors, having had many battles with the Sioux, sent scouts out ahead. The scouts discovered the ambush the Sioux had set up. The Sac sent runners to other Sac villages for help. When the Sioux saw that the ambush wasn't going to work, they retreated up to the top of the bluff on the north side of the mouth of this creek–planning to sneak back north early in the morning. But the next morning, the Sioux found that the Sac warriors had them hemmed in. Now they had a choice: face the Sac in battle or try to swim across the Mississippi River. But the Sac had canoes ready if they tried that. The Sioux set up their defense on the bluff the best they could. When the Sac attacked, they had a four to one advantage. When the battle was over, all the Sioux warriors were dead. The Sac scalped them and threw them off the bluff.

Many years later when the French fur traders stopped here, they found all these sun-bleached skulls and bones. So they named the creek "Tete du Morts" creek.

It is interesting to note that the Coast Guard navigation aid located on an island just across the river from where these bones were was named by the river pilots "Deadmans".

**Royal Mines of Spain**

Julien Dubuque, a French Canadian known to the Indians as "Little Night", while working at the French trading post at Prairie du Chien in the 1780's, learned about the lead ore deposits in the Catfish Creek area. This was west of the Mississippi River. But there was a problem. No white man was allowed to settle in the Indian territory west of the Mississippi River-north of the Missouri River.

Finally, Julien Dubuque arranged a pow-wow with the village Indian chief. It was held on the bank of Catfish Creek. Julien Dubuque requested permission to mine lead in their territory. The chief flatly refused. So, as last resort, Julien set up a bit of magic. While they were all sitting around the counsel fire talking, two of Julien's partners went up around the bend of the creek and poured a barrel of turpentine into the creek. Julien told the Indians that if they wouldn't allow him to mine lead in their territory, he would burn up their Mississippi River. He took a flaming stick from the counsel fire and threw it into the creek. The entire creek was ablaze. The terrified Indians conceded to all Julien Dubuque asked.

A year before George Washington was President-September 22, 1788, Julien Dubuque staked his claim on the west bank of the Mississippi River–twenty miles long, nine miles wide. In 1796, while the Louisiana Territory was under Spanish rule, the Spanish Government recognized Julien Dubuque's claim. That is why the area is called the "Royal Mines

*Julian Dubuque's tomb on a bluff in The Royal Mines of Spain Park overlooking the Mississippi River at Dubuque, Iowa. Courtesy Murphy Library, U.W.-LaCrosse.*

of Spain". Julien Dubuque worked his lead mines for twenty-two years. He built a home in Catfish Creek Indian Village and married Potose, the Indian chief's daughter. He died there in Catfish Valley in 1810.

### Blacksmith Slough

Around 1825, a French Canadian half-breed who had been taught the blacksmith trade, set up his blacksmith shop on a large island in the backwater slough across the Mississippi River from Homer, Minnesota. He did a lot of work for the Winnebago and Fox Indians. When Chief Black Hawk went on the warpath in 1832, this half-breed left his blacksmith shop on that island out in that slough and joined up with Chief Black Hawk, leaving his anvil, forge, and his other tools and equipment there. He never returned to his blacksmith shop. It is believed that he was killed in one of the battles.

The river pilots called it "Blacksmith Slough" even before the Black Hawk Wars. Now if you check the upper Mississippi River chart at mile 718.8, you will find a Coast Guard navigation aid with the name, "Blacksmith Slough".

### Jag Farm Island

One of the few private islands on the upper

Mississippi River is located across the river from Winona, Minnesota at mile 726.5. It has some interesting history of how it got its name.

On the U.S. Government charts, it is called Island 71. But that is not what the local river people call it.

During Prohibition back in the 1920's, there was a small farm on that island. The farmer had a still hidden on the island which he used to make "moonshine". Well, it didn't take long before the local fishermen out fishing in the river to discover what the farmer was doing. So when they went fishing, they would usually stop at the island and visit with this farmer. After that jug of "white lightning" was passed around a few times, the fishermen by the time they left had a pretty good jag on. It didn't take long before the fishermen started calling that island, "Jag Farm". To this day, the local river people call that island, "Jag Farm Island".

*Str. "Mollie McPike", 1864-1871, wood hull, stern-wheel, built at Madison, Ind. 180 x 27 x 5, steam engines 18 inches in diameter with a 5.5 foot stroke. On Nov. 8, 1871, it sank and was destroyed at Turner's Landing. Courtesy Murphy Library, U.W.-LaCrosse.*

*Str. "Phil Sheridan", 1866-1876, wood hull, side-wheel, built in Cincinnati, Ohio. 227 x 36.5 x 6, steam engines 22 inches in diameter with a 7 foot stroke, 4 boilers. In 1876, while being hauled out for repairs at LaCrosse, Wisc., the cradles let go and sank the boat. The boat was raised, dismantled and the machinery sold. Courtesy Murphy Library, U.W.-LaCrosse.*

During this same Prohibition period, just up the river a few miles on an island across the river from Fountain City, Wisconsin, a colorful lady character by the name of Mary and her party girls operated a speakeasy and served "bath tub gin". The local river people called her island, "Catfish Mary's".

**Beef Slough**

During the fall of year 1854 when the river was low, a paddlewheel steamboat with about 300 head of cattle on board for the army at Fort Snelling got stuck on a sand bar on the upper Mississippi River-no more than a mile above Alma, Wisconsin. The Captain had

*Str. "Red Wing", 1870-1882, wood hull, side-wheel, built at Brownsville, Pa. 245 x 35 x 6, steam engines 20 inches in diameter, working 11 foot buckets. It was dismantled in 1882. Courtesy Winona County Historical Society.*

the crew put off all the beef cattle over on the islands close by to lighten the paddlewheel steamboat so they could work themselves off the sand bar. After they got the paddlewheel steamboat off the sand bar and passed over it, the crew went ashore on the islands and rounded up all the cattle they could find. But quite a few strays were never found. For several years after that, in the early winter after the back water slough had frozen over, the settlers living in Alma, Wisconsin, would form a party of men and round up some of the stray beef cattle and butcher them for their winter meat supply. This is why the river pilots call this part of Nelson Bottoms, "Beef Slough".

*St. Anthony Falls in the Early 1800's.*
*Courtesy Winona County Historical Society.*

*Note the design of the early carbon arc search light on this steamboat.*
*Courtesy Winona County Historical Society.*

**Saint Anthony Falls**

Saint Anthony Falls is located at Minneapolis, Minnesota. In 1680, when Father Hennepin saw it, the falls was a mile further down the river than it is now. It was retreating about 4 feet a year until in the 1930's when the Army Engineers stabilized it where it is now.

**Search Light**

The first time a paddlewheel steamboat used an electric carbon arc searchlight was in 1875. It wasn't until the 1970's that there was a bulb light that could equal the light of the carbon arc.

**Planters Punch**

A bartender working at a bar in Planters Hotel in St. Louis is credited with the honor of creating this mixed drink. He combined a fruit punch with Southern Comfort and named it after the hotel, "Planters Punch".

**One Buck = One Dollar**

The term, one buck, got its start in the fur trader days. A deer skin was called a buckskin. When an Indian brought his buckskins in to trade, and wanted to trade for a knife, he would ask how many bucks for the knife. Since buckskins were worth one dollar and the knife was worth six dollars, the fur trader would answer, six bucks. Sometimes it was bought with four buckskins and two dollars. One dollar was one buck.

**Indian Slaves**

Yes, the American Indian tribes had slaves. These were usually prisoners captured in a raid of an enemy Indian village. The American Indian had a very interesting slave-freeing system. If a slave would go into battle with his owner and kill one of the enemy, the slave got his freedom.

**Mississippi River Mayflies**

Each summer, sometime between the last week of June to the middle of July, a flying insect hatches on the upper Mississippi River by the millions. This insect is called the mayfly. Other names for this insect are shad flies, willow bugs, fish flies, mormon flies, and love bugs.

The mayfly begins its life as a small egg on the bottom of the Mississippi River in the mud. When the water temperature is right, the nymph hatches as a small worm with a mouth, living on the river bottom

*Mayfly.*

eating small water plants and algae. This worm will live on the river bottom for anywhere from a few weeks to 3 years.

When river conditions are just right, the worm floats to the surface and becomes an adult mayfly with wings, six legs, but no mouth.

Once an adult, the mayfly will live for only about 24 hours. In this short time, the female has to find a mate. She does this by flying, doing a love dance to attract a male lover. They mate in mid-air. The male has to fly upside down to mate with his honey. Immediately after mating, the female mayfly lays her eggs on the water, which sink to the bottom, and the female dies. The male flies off to a bush or a tree. If it is dark, he will fly towards a light. The male mayfly also dies in a few hours. During this period, fishing is very poor on the river.

**Jazz Music**

The New Orleans style dance music got its name, "jazz music" from the Streckfus paddlewheel steamboat, "J.S.". The "J.S." had a talented group of New Orleans musicians on board playing this New Orleans style dance music. This style of dance music became very popular, and soon other bands picked it up and were playing it at dances.

At first, it was called, "J.S. Music". It wasn't long before "J.S." became "Jazz". That is why today it is called "Jazz Music".

**River Pilot Abraham Lincoln**

Yes, President Abraham Lincoln in his youth did some river piloting. I don't recall the date Lincoln piloted a flat boat loaded with farm produce down the Sagamon River into the Illinois to the Mississippi River all the way to New Orleans. It was when he was in New Orleans on this trip that he witnessed a slave auction which set him against slavery.

He also helped a captain of a small paddlewheel steamboat get over a dam on the Sagamon River during a low water period. Abraham Lincoln held a patent on a system to increase floatation of a steamboat so it

*Str. "J.S.", 1901-1910, wood hull, stern-wheel, built at Jefferson, Ind. for Streckfus Line. It was the first paddlewheel steamboat designed and built just for day excursion use. 175 x 33 x 5.5, steam engines 16 inches in diameter with a 6 foot stroke, 2 boilers. It burned and sank by Bad Axe Island just below Genoa, Wisc. in 1910. Courtesy Winona County Historical Society.*

*Str. "J.S." Main Lounge.  Courtesy Murphy Library, U.W.-LaCrosse.*

*Selecting a name for a boat can be a challenge. Paddlewheel steamboat owners started a new naming system. They took the old name and added a number to it. Courtesy Winona County Historical Society.*

could get over a sandbar. His system was to lower into the water hollow logs on both sides of the hull when needed to add the additional floatation and reduce the draft of the vessel so it would clear the sandbar.

I am sure this river background helped Lincoln get selected to represent the railroad in the suit by the paddlewheel steamboat companies against the railroads building bridges across the Mississippi River. This was after the paddlewheel steamboat, "Effie Afton" hit the first railroad bridge built across the Mississippi River at Rock Island, Illinois.

### Sunday, a Day of Rest

Captain Orrin Smith, owner and captain of the paddlewheel steamboat, "Nominee" was a Christian. Since Sunday was a day of rest, he would tie his boat off wherever it was at midnight Saturday. It didn't move again until after midnight Sunday.

On Sunday, Captain Orrin Smith had a church service on board. If there was a preacher on board, he was asked to conduct church services. If not, Captain Smith would conduct one himself.

Most paddlewheel steamboats that carried passengers held a church service on Sunday, but there were only a few that would tie off like Captain Orrin Smith did.

### Twin Stern Paddlewheels

Today there are several paddlewheel excursion boats operating on the rivers with twin paddlewheels. They give the pilot the same added maneuverability as twin props on a power boat. Of course, the sidewheel steamboats had 2 paddlewheels and had a maneuverability advantage over a stern wheel steamboat. But the sternwheel steamboat could operate in rivers of shallow water.

The first paddlewheel steamboat to use twin stern paddlewheels was the paddlewheel steamboat, "Aunt Letty". This boat was built on the Ohio River in 1855. "Aunt Letty" had four high pressure steam engines to operate the twin paddlewheels.

### Boat Names with II, III, etc.

Naming a second boat the same as the first boat got started by the owners of the paddlewheel steamboats on the rivers. Because of the need of shallow draft to operate on the river, the paddlewheel steamboats were built of light wood construction to reduce weight.

There was also always unpredictable changes on the river that would cause the destruction of a boat. Also, if a fire got started, there was no stopping it as everything was built of wood.

*Flatboat, wooden barge, floating down the river. River pilots called them "broad horns" because of their long oars.*
*Courtesy Winona County Historical Society.*

Paddlewheel steamboats of the mid-1800's lasted only 3 to 5 years. When a boat was destroyed, the engines, boilers, and everything possible was salvaged and put into a new boat. Paddlewheel steamboats in the mid-1800's were very good money makers.

The owners, instead of trying to think of a new name, just took the old one and added a number after it. Captain Thomas P. Leathers had several "Natchez" built. The last one was "Natchez VIII".

### Steamboat Whistle

The first steamboat to have a steam whistle was a paddlewheel steamboat, "Revenue" in 1840.

### Broad-Horns

Broad-horns is a riverman's term for the flatboat floating down the river. These were unpowered wooden barges that floated with the current down the river. To steer these flatboats, they had several long oars, called sweeps, that extended out both sides of the flatboats (Broad-horns).

When the flatboats (Broad-horns) got to New Orleans, they sold the farm produce they brought. Then they took the flatboat apart and sold the lumber. This lumber was used to build many homes in New Orleans. Two thousand, seven hundred flatboats

arrived at New Orleans in 1847.

### Elsah, Illinois

At first, the river pilots called this, "Jersey's Landing". Then in 1853, General James Semple bought up the land in this valley between these bluffs, plotted it out, and filed the survey with the name, Elsah.

Elsah, Illinois, is the first entire community to be listed on the National Register of Historical Places. Elsah has been restored to its 1860 lifestyle.

### Buffalo, Iowa

Captain Bengerman Clark had a homestead across the river at Andalusia, Illinois. After the Black Hawk War of 1832, Iowa Territory was open for homesteading. Captain Clark staked a claim across the river in Iowa, surveyed, plotted and named it Buffalo. Then to make it easy for settlers to get to the land he had for sale, he built a ferry. But unlike the other ferries on the Mississippi River at that time, he was the first to build a ferry large enough to take a double team and wagon across the river at one time.

With the help of Captain Clark's ferry, the village started out with a boom and was one of the fastest growing villages in Iowa until 1856. The railroad built

*Paddlewheel steamboat "Delta Queen" on an excursion cruise.*

*Bird's eye view of Quad Cities: Davenport and Bettendorf, Iowa, on the left;*
*Rock Island and Moline, Illinois on the right with Arsenal Island.*
*Courtesy Rock Island Preservation Commission.*

a bridge across the Mississippi River between Rock Island, Illinois, and Davenport, Iowa. That year, Buffalo's growth came to a halt and Davenport, Iowa, took over.

### Campbell's Island

During the War of 1812 with the British, the U.S. Army sent Lt. Campbell and his company of troops up the Mississippi River in keel boats in the summer of 1814.

At Campbell's Island, just off the shore of East Moline, Illinois, Lt. Campbell made a deal with Chief Black Hawk. For two barrels of whiskey, Chief Black Hawk let Lt. Campbell set up a base camp on the Island.

Shortly after the whiskey was gone, Chief Black Hawk and his braves went up to Prairie du Chien, which at that time was in the hands of the British. The Indians told the British of Lt. Campbell's location, and offered to help the British capture Lt. Campbell's troops.

On July 19, 1814, the British and Indian braves surprised Lt. Campbell's troops. They had to make a quick retreat back down the Mississippi River leaving one of their keel boats on the Island. There is now a park on this island with 4 cannon and a monument in the memory of the soldiers who lost their lives in that battle. The cannon date back to the Revolutionary War.

## Pelican and Credit Island

After Lt. Campbell's defeat, Maj. Zachary Taylor was sent up the Mississippi River to capture the fort the British held at Prairie du Chien. He had under his command 334 troops.

Maj. Zachary Taylor set up a base camp on the small island, Pelican, and on the upper end of Credit Island. But before the troops could get good fortifications built, the British, with the help of Chief Black Hawk's braves, attacked on September 5, 1814. The U.S. Army troops were defeated, but were allowed to return down river because the British had run out of ammunition.

This was the only battle Maj. Zachary Taylor lost while an officer in the U.S. Army. It is not recorded how many Indian braves took part in the attack, but the British had only 60 troops in this attack.

## Arsenal Island
## Rock Island, Illinois

Arsenal Island is 2 1/2 miles long, 3/4 mile wide and 946 acres in all. Fort Armstrong was built here in 1816. After the Civil War, the whole island became a military reservation.

Anyone interested in early American history could easily spend a week on this island. From the river the first thing one can see is the clock tower. This building and tower are built of stone from a quarry up the river at LeClaire, Iowa. Most of the labor came from Confederate prisoners that were held here in the prisoner of war camp on the island. The clock has four faces. Each face is 12 feet in diameter. The hands are 5 and 6 feet long. The pendulum is 30 feet long. The bell weighs 3,500 pounds. It is a manual clock and has to be wound once a week.

During the Civil War, Confederate prisoners also built 8 other quarry stone buildings that are used to manufacture and store Army equipment. Now the Army has 200 buildings on the island that are used for manufacturing, testing, and storing of military equipment. This employs 4,000 to 6,000 civilian employees.

George Davenport came here in 1816 when Fort Armstrong was built. He staked a claim on 160 acres of the 946 acres on the island. In 1833, he built a nine room mansion home along the shore facing the main channel. This home has been restored and is now open for public tours.

On July 4, 1845, seven armed men entered Davenport's home. It was rumored he had hidden $20,000 in gold. They tortured Col. Davenport and finally killed him. All they got was $300. They were later caught and tried in a Rock Island court. Three of the men were hanged.

The poet, Longfellow, wrote a poem about an Indian maiden that fell in love with a white man. That poem was based on the true-to-life love affair between a U.S. Army doctor based on Arsenal Island, Dr. John Gale, and a local Indian girl, Niconmi (voice of water). Longfellow changed her name in his poem to Minnehaha (laughing waters). Dr. John Gale died and was buried here on Arsenal Island in 1834. Niconmi died in 1888 and also was buried on the island.

Besides Davenport's home, there are several stone homes along the shore of the main channel of the river. The first one up from Davenport's home, and the largest, is quarters for the Commander of the island. It is known as "Quarters One" and built in 1870. This home has had the honor of having some United States Presidents staying here while they visited the Quad Cities. The wrought iron fence around the house was made from melted down old Civil War cannon balls.

From "Quarters One" up the shore, each house is smaller than its neighbor. The lower the officer rank, the smaller quarters he gets.

The land that is a golf course now was the prisoner of war site during the Civil War. After that, it was a polo ground. Every Sunday afternoon all summer long, the Army officers played polo. The polo games ended with World War II.

There are three military cemeteries on the island, National Cemetery, Confederate Cemetery, and Ft. Armstrong Cemetery. Confederate prisoners of war that died here during the Civil War were buried in their own cemetery. In Ft. Armstrong Cemetery, there are soldiers and early pioneers buried and was used until 1865 when the National Cemetery was opened.

As a memorial to the father of automatic weapons, they have the John M. Browning Museum on the island. This museum has a large collection of military weapons dating back to the Pre-Revolutionary War period.

### Pearl Wizard of the West

During the period of upper Mississippi River history when the river clam shells were being used to make buttons, Mr. W.L. Gardner of LeClaire, Iowa, made a small fortune buying up the pearls and slugs that the clammers found when removing the meat from the clam shell.

The pearls from the Mississippi clam were just as valuable as a pearl from an oyster. The difference between a slug and a pearl was its shape. The pearl, of

*Green Tree Hotel. Courtesy Winona County Historical Society.*

course, was perfectly round. The slug was irregular in shape. Many slugs ended up on a ring. These rings can still be found at estate sales in towns along the Mississippi River.

Mr. Gardner would buy these slugs and pearls from the clammers. When he had accumulated a good supply, he would make a trip to New York City and sell them to the jewelers there.

He bought slugs for $2.50 to $3.00 an ounce. For pearls, he would pay anywhere from $100 to $3,000 each. His best buy was a pink pearl. He bought it for $1,000 and sold it in New York for $12,000.

### Green Tree Hotel

When the paddlewheel steamboats or log rafts would stop at LeClaire, Iowa, and wait for a rapids pilot to board and guide them through the Rock Island Rapids, the deck crew (roustabouts, sometimes called roosters) would go uptown to a saloon for a drink or two. But most of the time, it was more than two. By the time they got back to the river, their boat or raft was gone. Now their money was gone. So they would just camp out under the big elm tree on the river bank and wait for another boat or raft that needed crew replacements–because it had lost crew members to the uptown saloons when they stopped to take on a rapids pilot. Good old Yankee humor dubbed their open air

lodging, "The Green Tree Hotel". This rock elm was 65 feet high with a branch spread of 110 feet. It succumbed to Dutch Elm disease in 1964. A section of its trunk was saved and used as part of The Green Tree Hotel Monument on the river front.

### Buffalo Bill Cody

When Buffalo Bill's name comes up, we place him out on the Western plains. But did you know his life began on the upper Mississippi River? As a youth, he lived in LeClaire, Iowa. He was born there on February 26, 1846.

While just a young boy, he rode for the Pony Express. He was an Army scout for a short while. Then when the Kansas Pacific Railroad needed a hunter to supply buffalo meat for their construction crew, Buffalo Bill took on the job. In an 18-month period, he shot 4,280 buffalo. After that, he became owner and showman of

*Buffalo Bill Cody, born in LeClaire, Iowa. Courtesy Murphy Library, U.W.-LaCrosse.*

*Paddlewheel steamboat "J. M. Richtman".*
*Courtesy Winona County Historical Society.*

Buffalo Bill's Wild West Show.

On the river bank at LeClaire, Iowa, they have the Buffalo Bill Museum. Next to the Museum is a paddlewheel steamboat museum, the paddlewheel, "Lone Star". "Lone Star" was the last wooden hull paddlewheel steamboat to operate on the Mississippi River. It was built in 1869 and the "Lone Star" became a steamboat museum in LeClaire, Iowa, in 1968.

### Wapsipinincon River

Between Princeton and Comanche, Iowa, the Wapsipinincon River enters the Mississippi River. It's an Indian name. Translated it means, "river where you find white potatoes". River pilots shorten it to "Wapsie". When this was French territory, the fur trappers called it the White Swan River. Hundreds of white swans nested by the river. When Father Marquette and Joliet explored the Mississippi River, they visited a Sac Indian village here.

### Red Brick Hotel

In 1856, all of the business buildings in Clinton, Iowa, were wooden frame buildings since Clinton was known as "Saw Dust Town". But a modern five-story red brick hotel changed that. This modern hotel had hot and cold running water in every room. Attached to the back of the hotel was a five-story red brick outhouse.

### Grave Robbers

In 1875, Fulton, Illinois had a very notorious citizen, Ben Boyd. It seems that the states of Illinois and Iowa were being flooded with counterfeit money. Federal agents were called in on the case.

Ben Boyd, a well-to-do man living in Fulton turned out to be the leader of this gang of counterfeiters. Federal agents arrested him. He was tried and sent to jail. His pals felt that they should at least attempt to free him. They had a great idea. Over in Springfield, Illinois, President Abraham Lincoln was buried. It was decided to dig up Lincoln's body and hold it for ransom for the release of their leader, Ben Boyd. The Feds got wind of this plan, caught them in the act, and put them all in jail.

Because of this threat, Abraham Lincoln's grave has been encased in 40 feet of concrete reinforced with steel railroad track to discourage any such acts in the future.

### Egg Business

In Sabula, Iowa, the early settlers' main source of income was from the sale of eggs. This egg business was not like the chicken farms of today. In the spring

*Str. "Keokuk", 1858-1866, side-wheel, wood hull, built at Brownsville, Pa.*
*177 x 27.5 x 5, steam engines 20 inches in diameter with a 5 1/2 foot stroke, 3 boilers.*
*Master Capt. Silas, Pilot Capt. E.V. Holcomb. A Northwestern Union Packet Line boat.*
*Courtesy Winona County Historical Society.*

of the year, the settlers would go out in the back waters of the Mississippi River and collect wagon loads of swan eggs. They sold these eggs to the paddlewheel steamboats.

## Captain's Home

Cruising on the Mississippi River past the city of Savanna, Illinois, you will see up on a hill, a two-story brick home. Up on the roof is a room with large windows overlooking the river. Some people call this room a cupola, others a river widow's lookout.

After Captain Cooley retired, he had this home built up on the hill to avoid the danger of flood. Then, so he had a good unobstructed view of the Mississippi, he had that special room built on the roof. In his retirement years, he spent many days up there watching the activity on the Mississippi River.

*Captain Cooley's retirement home at Savanna, Ill.*
*Courtesy Murphy Library, U.W.-LaCrosse.*

## Blind Bends

Four miles above Savanna, Illinois, by Keller's Landing Light, the channel is very narrow and has a 90 degree blind bend. This is no place for towboats to meet. It is such a tight bend that it was even close for the paddlewheel steamboats meeting in the bend.

In 1855, two paddlewheel steamboats got too close when they met in this bend. "Dr. Franklin" was coming down the river, making good time. Coming up river with a full head of steam was the "Galena". Right in this bend they met. Neither pilot saw the other boat more than seconds before they crashed. "Galena" rammed the "Dr. Franklin" just forward of the boilers. "Dr. Franklin" sank at once. Shortly after this, because of this accident, Congress passed a law that requires a boat to blow its whistle when coming to a blind bend. This law is still in the Inland Rules of the Road. Rule #34 paragraph (e). Now days, you will find that commercial towboats use channel 13 on their marine radio to communicate with each other when nearing a narrow channel or blind bend in the river.

## Horse Thieves

Now days they steal cars. In the frontier days, it was horses.

*Paddlewheel steamboat "Gem City". Courtesy Winona County Historical Society.*

Around Dubuque, in Iowa and Illinois, there was a very active gang of horse thieves. Brown, the owner of the Brown Hotel in the river village of Bellevue, Iowa, was the leader of the gang.

After some searching, the sheriff found the trail of the horse thieves led to the Brown Hotel. He also learned there were 17 well-armed horse thieves holed up in the hotel. Since he and his deputy were outnumbered, the sheriff formed a posse of 40 citizens to capture the gang of horse thieves. They surrounded the Brown Hotel. There was a lot of shooting. Four of the gang and four of the posse were killed. It was a standoff until the sheriff set fire to the hotel. The thirteen remaining horse thieves were captured.

Then the citizens had to decide. Should they hang them or horse whip the horse thieves? They took a vote using beans dropped in a hat: white bean for hanging, colored bean for whipping. The colored beans won. The horse thieves were whipped, put on a raft, and set adrift down the river.

## Badger State

In the mid 1800's, Galena, Illinois, and Cassville, Wisconsin, were the leading shippers of lead down the Mississippi River. Galena is a Latin word for lead sulfide. James D. Bourne started mining lead sulfide out of his Vinegar Hill Mine in 1832. Later, he found a new deposit of lead sulfide at Potosi, Wisconsin. He sold his Viniger Hill Mine and moved to Potosi.

By 1850, there were 10,000 lead miners in the Cassville and Potosi, Wisconsin, area. Most of these miners lived in the lead mine shaft with their families. When the sun came up in the morning, the miners and their families would come out of the mines all over the hillside. When visitors saw this in the mornings, it looked like a hillside of badgers coming out of their dens to sun themselves. It didn't take long before Wisconsin was called the "Badger State".

## Shot Tower

Along the river bank at Dubuque, Iowa, there is a tall brick chimney standing all by itself. It is listed in the National Register of Historical Buildings. But it is not a chimney. It is listed as a shot tower.

A shot tower was used to make lead balls for muzzle loading rifles. Melted lead was poured through a screen on top of the tower. As the droplets of lead fell, they would cool into round balls, lead shot. The lead shot was collected, sized, and sold to the Army and to hunters.

This shot tower was built in 1856. It is 70 feet high. With all the lead mines close by and the Mississippi River to ship the lead shot by paddlewheel steamboat, this made an ideal location. Most of the lead shot for the Civil War came from here.

During the Civil War, this shot tower was making a good profit. During the Civil War, the man that built the shot tower made another profit by selling this shot tower. But before the buyer would buy the shot tower, he had to agree not to build another shot tower. He agreed. That didn't stop him from making lead shot. He bought an old lead mine shaft and started making lead shot, having the lead drops fall down the shaft and cool into round lead shot.

*What looks like a tall smoke stack is the historical 1856 shot tower at Dubuque, Iowa. It was used to make lead balls for muzzle loading rifles during the Civil War. Courtesy Dubuque Chamber of Commerce.*

## Brass Bowl

A fur trapper, Robert Grant, did his trapping around Prairie du Chien and Cassville, Wisconsin. He trapped and bought furs from the Indians on his own. He lived off the land as he worked the trap lines. He cooked his food in a brass bowl. After he had eaten, he would wash the brass bowl and put it on his head under his fur hat.

One day as Robert Grant was making his way to the trading post at Prairie du Chien with a heavy pack of furs on his back, an Indian brave attacked him with a toma-hawk. He hit Robert Grant in the head. There was a

*Str. "Rob Roy", 1866-1880, wood hull, side-wheel, built at Madison, Ind. 235 x 41 x 6, steam engines 26 inches in diameter with a 7 foot stroke, paddlewheels 28 feet in diameter working 14 foot buckets. It sank in 1874, was raised and repaired. It sank again in 1880, salvaged and dismantled. Courtesy Murphy Library, U.W.-LaCrosse.*

loud clank.  Robert Grant staggered, but didn't go down.  The Indian brave fled in fear.

Robert Grant became a hero.  Everyone wanted to see his dented brass cooking bowl he had under his hat.  They honored Robert Grant by naming a county after him–Grant County, Wisconsin.

### Bushwhacking

The term, bushwhacking, goes back to the Mississippi River keel boat era.  On their trips up the Mississippi when the river was in flood stage, the keel boats would leave the main channel and work their way up through the back waters where there was less current.  When they did this, the crew would grab branches of trees and bushes to pull the keel boat up the river.  The rivermen call this, "bushwhacking" up the river.  Since then, this term has been used to describe many other activities.

### Mark Twain

This is the name Samuel Clemens used when he wrote his famous stories–a term he took from the paddlewheel steamboats.  It was a term used when they were slowly working the boat through a shallow stretch of the river.

To determine the depth of the river, they would use a line (rope) with a weight on its end, usually made of lead.  It was called a "lead line".  This lead line was marked off in 1/4 fathoms.  One fathom is 6 feet.  The man on the bow working the lead line would call out the depth to the mate standing on the cabin deck roof.  The mate would call the depth to the pilot.

If you look up the word, "twain" in the dictionary, you will find it means two.  So "mark twain" means two fathoms (12 feet).  When the pilot heard "mark twain", he had cleared the shallow stretch.  Now the boat was in deep water.  He could relax and ring his engineer for full ahead.

### Looking Backwards

At LeClaire, Iowa, the Mississippi River makes a 90 degree turn to the west and flows 43 miles west to Muscatine, Iowa.  At Muscatine, it turns back south.

There is an American Indian legend about this.  It said:  The Mississippi River, on its way to the Gulf of Mexico, and after it had gone through the northern bluff territory–it was so beautiful the Mississippi River turned to have a second look before continuing its way down to the Gulf of Mexico.

### Big Cave

When you are in a boat going by Clayton, Iowa, just below the town in a limestone bluff close to the river bank, you will see a large cave. It's large enough to drive a truck into. This cave is really a mine, a silica sand mine. They mine a type of pure silica sand that has not been found any place else in the world. They mine and ship this silica sand to companies all over the world.

This mine has also been designated as a fall-out shelter by the U.S. Government. The mine is large enough to shelter 40,000 people.

### Wisconsin River

Just below Prairie du Chien, Wisconsin, the Wisconsin River enters the Mississippi River. This is the river Father Marquette and Louis Joliet canoed down in 1673 and located the Mississippi River.

Shortly after that, the Wisconsin River became part of the French Great Empire Trade Route. It was the major trade route for the French Voyageurs who were fur traders. The French Voyageurs would take their canoes loaded with furs up the Wisconsin River, portage about 2 miles to the Fox River, down the Fox River which flows east and north into Lake Michigan at Green Bay, then on to the St Lawrence River.

In the late 1860's, the Army Engineers improved navigation on the Fox and Wisconsin Rivers so paddlewheel steamboats could operate on those rivers. Then in 1875-76, the Army Engineers built a canal between the Wisconsin River and the Fox at Portage, Wisconsin. This Federal waterway was in operation until 1950. Because of a lack of commercial use, the system was disbanded by the Federal Government. Some of the sections of the Fox River between Neenah, Menasha, and Green Bay have been taken over by the State of Wisconsin.

### Pike's Peak

Yes, Pike's Peak is on the Mississippi River. If you don't believe it, look at an Iowa map. You will find it just about 2 miles below McGregor, Iowa, across the river from where the Wisconsin River enters the Mississippi.

Of course, this isn't the 14,000 foot mountain that is in the state of Colorado. This Pike's Peak is only a limestone bluff about 1,000 feet above sea level along the Iowa bank of the Mississippi River.

When Lt. Pike was sent out to explore and map the upper Mississippi River in 1805, Lt. Pike named this bluff and marked it on his map as a good location for a fort. The fort was never built.

*The 10 Marching Bears in the Effigy Mounds National Park,*
*located along the Mississippi River between Marquette and Lansing, Iowa.*
*Courtesy Iowa Conservation Commission.*

### Effigy Burial Mounds

Along the Mississippi River, there are many burial sites. Most are just conical in shape. The Effigy Burial Mounds are located on a bluff in a National Park that overlooks the Mississippi River.

In this park, there are 191 prehistoric burial mounds that date back to 500 years before the birth of Jesus Christ. Twenty-nine of these mounds are in the shape of a bird or a bear. One of the largest is in the shape of a bear. The bear is 137 feet long, 3 1/2 feet high and from the front paws to the top of its shoulder is 70 feet. There is also a group of 10 bear mounds that has been named "The 10 Marching Bears".

The National Effigy Mounds Park is located 3 miles up river from Marquette, Iowa. The park is open to the public with tours year round.

### Mt. Hosmer Lookout

On the north side of Lansing, Iowa's, business district along the Mississippi River bank is a limestone bluff, Mt. Hosmer Lookout.

Miss Hosmer was a well-known artist during the mid-1800's. In the summer of 1851, she bought passage on Captain Orrin Smith's paddlewheel steamboat, "Senator".

One day on this trip in June, 1851, the "Senator" made a wood stop at Lansing, Iowa. Since it was going to take a couple hours or so to load the twenty cords of wood, Miss Hosmer went ashore for a stroll around the village. Finding a trail that went up to the

*Lansing, Iowa, with Mt. Hosmer in the background. Courtesy Murphy Library, U.W.-LaCrosse.*

top of the bluff, she climbed to the top and was rewarded with a beautiful view of the Mississippi Valley.

When she returned to the boat, she told Captain Smith about her stroll and climb to the top of the bluff and the beautiful view. Captain Smith was impressed to hear that Miss Hosmer had climbed to the top of the bluff. He gave it her name. To impress Miss Hosmer, he listed the bluff on his river chart as Mt. Hosmer.

Now a road has been constructed up the bluff so tourists can drive up to Mt. Hosmer to view the Mississippi Valley.

### Battle Island

Four miles below the Minnesota-Iowa border, along the Wisconsin shore of the Mississippi River, you will find Black Hawk Memorial Park and Battle Island. Here by the river and up into the bluffs close by is where the Black Hawk War of 1832 came to an end.

The U.S. Army had hired Captain Throckmorton's paddlewheel steamboat, "Warrior". They put a 6-pound cannon on the bow and 40 troops under the command of Captain Jefferson Davis on board. They sent the "Warrior" up the Mississippi River from Rock Island with orders to cut off Chief Black Hawk's escape across the river.

The Army then sent General Atkinson, in command of 600 troops, by land in pursuit of Chief Black Hawk and his braves.

Chief Black Hawk, unaware of the cannon and troops on the paddlewheel steamboat sent the older men, women, and children to safety across the river. Very few succeeded. The cannon and riflemen on the "Warrior" killed most of them as they were swimming across the river.

Chief Black Hawk then saw he was out-gunned and trapped. He and his braves surrendered.

### Winneshiek Landing

DeSoto, Wisconsin, is on land that was a campsite of a Winnebago Indian tribe under the leadership of Chief Winneshiek, (Wee-nes-shiek). Part of the town of DeSoto has been built over the tribal burial grounds. Chief Wee-nes-shiek was not buried there, but up on a nearby bluff.

The river pilots called this, Winneshiek Landing, until the village decided to incorporate and honor the Spanish explorer who located the Mississippi River in 1541, DeSoto.

During the summer of 1827, some of Chief Wee-nes-shiek's young braves got into an argument with a keel boat crew. Before the argument was over, one of the young braves was killed. Later on that summer, another keel boat that was owned by O.H. Perry had the misfortune of grounding on a sand bar a few miles up river from Winneshiek Landing. Chief Wee-nes-shiek took advantage of this opportunity to avenge the death of that young brave. He and 37 of his warriors attacked Perry's keel boat while it was stuck on the sand bar. By the time the attack was over, 4 of Perry's crew and 7 Indians were dead. Since then, this section from Lock and Dam 8 to the Minnesota-Iowa border has been known as "Bad Axe".

Chief Wee-nes-shiek's daughter became ill in 1876. Dr. Powell in LaCrosse, Wisconsin, treated and healed her. Shortly after, the Chief made Dr. Powell, chief medicine man, "White Beaver". Four years later, Dr. Powell was elected mayor of the town of LaCrosse, Wisconsin.

## Bad Axe

Just above Lock and Dam 8 on the Mississippi River is the town of Genoa, Wisconsin. This landing was called Bad Axe. Then, in 1869, a group of Italian immigrants settled here and changed the name. They named it after the town they left in Italy-Genoa.

Dairyland Power has one of their coal-fired electric power plants here. After World War II, Dairyland Power built the first atomic energy steam electric gen-erator that produced electricity commercially here. It was a small plant in comparison to the nuclear plants built now. The building is still there. You can see it as you cruise by, but it has ceased operating. It was too small to operate economically.

## Coon Slough

Four miles above Genoa, Wisconsin, the main channel of the Mississippi River leaves the Wisconsin side of the valley and bends and twists through a maze of stump fields and small islands. Just as it turns towards Minnesota by the navigation aid, Warners Landing Light, lay the remains of three paddlewheel steamboats.

The first to sink here was the "Nominee" in 1854. It hit a snag in the river and sank. Two years later, 1856, the paddlewheel steamboat, "Lady Franklin" hit the same snag and sank very close by the "Nominee". Thirty-eight years later, 1894, the paddlewheel steam-boat, "Raindeer"–in the late summer during a very low water period–hit the wreckage of the "Lady Franklin" and sank. All three boats were damaged so badly they were beyond salvage value. Their remains still lay there in the mud at the bottom of the Mississippi River.

### Wild Kat Park

At Brownsville, Minnesota, before the bridge was built at LaCrosse, Wisconsin, there was a ferry operating across the river here. Its landing on the Minnesota side was at this park. It was a two-horse power ferry, that is, two real hay burners, real horses, on treadmills turning side paddlewheels. The operator named his rare ferry, "Wild Kat". He is the one that spelled cat with and "k", and it is still spelled that way at the park.

*Two horsepower WildKats Ferry at Brownsville, Minn. Courtesy Murphy Library, U.W.-LaCrosse.*

### Queen's Bluff

Between Dresbach, Minnesota, and Trempealeau, Wisconsin, on the Minnesota side of the Mississippi River is nature's highest stone face bluff overlooking the Mississippi River, 1,244 feet above sea level.

The bluff face is round and all around the bare stone face are pine trees that create the appearance of a green queen's crown. That is why the old river pilots named it Queen's Bluff.

Just over the valley from Queen's Bluff is another bluff almost as high, Menneowah Bluff. The local residents call this bluff, "Twin Bluffs" because of a big split down the middle of the top third of the bluff.

### Lost Canoe

One summer day in the 1830's while canoeing down the Mississippi River, a Sioux medicine chief having consumed too much of white man's fire water, became drowsy and stopped at a sand bar. He got out of his canoe, laid down in the shade of a tree, and went to sleep.

Before he woke, there was a slight rise in the river and his canoe with the medicine bag of healing charms and herbs drifted on down the river.

The canoe landed on Johnson's Point. Leonard

Johnson, a Swedish immigrant, had a woodyard on this point, selling cord wood to the paddlewheel steamboats. This point is located at the mouth of Homer Creek at Homer, Minnesota.

When Leonard Johnson saw the canoe with no one in it, he pulled it up on shore, saw the medicine bag, took it, and pushed the canoe back out in the river. It would drift on by, and the lost medicine bag could not be traced to him. His intentions were to sell the magic charms and herbs. He burned the medicine bag. Leonard did not know how serious an act this was. This could cause the Sioux Indian tribe to go on the war path.

William Bunnell, the owner of the trading post at Homer, learned that Leonard Johnson had the healing charms and herbs. He made arrangements for the return of the charms and herbs. But since Leonard Johnson had burned the

*William Bunnell built this home in the 1850's overlooking the Mississippi River at the village of Homer, Minn. A fur trader, he came up the river from LaCrosse, Wisc., set up his trading post in 1849. The home has been restored by the Winona County Historical Society. Courtesy Winona County Historical Society.*

medicine bag, he had to leave the territory or the Sioux would still scalp him.

**Sam Gordy's Slough**

Sam Gordy's Slough is the local rivermen's name of a Mississippi River back water across the river from Winona, Minnesota. You will not find that name on any chart or map. But if you talk to any local Winona fisherman, you may hear them speak of catching fish in Sam Gordy's Slough. The history behind this name goes back to 1865.

That is the year Sam Van Gorder started operating a ferry service on the river at Winona, Minnesota. The next year, 1866, with the help from the city of Winona, Sam built a road with several small bridges across the back water slough (Sam Gordy's).

Sam Van Gorder's ferry, the "Turtle" had 2 hulls, 70 feet long. The paddlewheel mounted between the hulls was steam-powered. It could carry 4 double teams across the river at once.

Two years after the road was built across the slough, 1868, Sam Van Gorder made a deal with a stagecoach company in Eau Claire, Wisconsin. Sam agreed to provide a horse barn at his ferry landing on the Wisconsin side for the stagecoach company-use free of charge. For the free use of this barn, the stage-coach company agreed to use Sam Van Gordon's ferry to cross the Mississippi River. This was the start of a mail run between Winona and Eau Claire.

In 1878, the ferry, "Turtle" burned. Sam Van Gorder had a new larger ferry built–95 feet by 35 feet–paddlewheel powered by steam. It could carry 12 double teams and also was named "Turtle". The city of Winona bought Sam's ferry in 1880 for $6,000 and gave Sam free rides for the rest of his life.

Then, in 1887, the city built a bridge across the back channel to Latch Island and installed a new cable ferry across the main channel. The city sold the "Turtle" back to Sam Van Gorder for $250. The cable ferry operated until the toll bridge was built in 1892.

The locals started calling that slough "Sam Gordy's" in 1865 when he started operating his ferry. I guess after 100 years, the name, Sam Gordy's Slough, will stick.

*Str. "Turtle", Sam Van Gorder's Ferry at Winona, Minn. Courtesy Winona County Historical Society.*

## Pig Island

There is an island off the shore of Fountain City, Wisconsin, in the Mississippi River called Pig Island. There is also a navigation aid called Pig Island.

This island got its name from the river pilots back when there was a creamery in Fountain City making butter from the local dairy farmers' cream. The

*Fountain City, Wisconsin's river front in the late 1800's.*
*Courtesy Winona County Historical Society.*

creamery operator raised hogs on that island. He had a pipeline laid along the river bottom to the island. The leftover buttermilk was pumped over to his hogs on the island. When the creamery closed down, so did the hog operation on the island. But the name stayed–Pig Island.

### Falling Rocks

Driving on the Great River Road along the Mississippi River, you see signs, "Watch out for Falling Rocks". Ever wonder how big these rocks will be? How about a 7 ton rock.

On midnight, April 5, 1901, high on Eagle Bluff overlooking the sleeping town of Fountain City, Wisconsin, on the Mississippi River, a large boulder, believed to weigh about 7 tons, became loosened by melting snow and started to tumble down the bluff side. It gained momentum, swerved, took a jump of 100 feet, landed, gained more momentum, bounded into the air, and crashed through the roof of Mr. and Mrs. Dubler's home. The house was demolished. The Dublers were sound asleep. They ended up in the basement with the 7 ton rock amid the ruins of the house. Mrs. Dubler was killed instantly. Mr. Dubler, who was blind, awakened to find himself buried under the ruins. The neighbors heard the crash and hurried to help. They could hear Mr. Dubler calling for help. After removing broken timbers and other rubble, Mr. Dubler was rescued with no broken bones, just bruises on his head and body.

*At midnight, April 5, 1901, a 7 ton rock tumbled down from the bluff above Fountain City, Wisc, demolished this house, killing Mrs. Dubler. Courtesy Winona County Historical Society.*

Mrs. Dubler's body was found crushed under the 7 ton rock.

### Mid-stream Delivery

Mid-stream fuel and grocery delivery of today for the river towboats got its start in 1839 at Holm's Landing.

Mr. Holms had a wood yard located on the Mississippi River where the town of Fountain City is now. Because there was no other reason to stop at his landing except to take on cord wood, his volume of sales to paddlewheel steamboats was very poor. He reasoned that if they didn't have to stop, he could get more sales. The answer was to build a wooden barge large enough to load 15 cords of wood on. Then when the paddlewheel steamboats got to his landing, all they had to do was catch a line to the cord wood barge and keep steaming up the river while the cord wood was loaded on board. After the barge was empty, it was released and it drifted back down the river to Holm's Landing, reloaded and waited for the next customer.

### U.S. Army Boat Yard

The U.S. Army Engineers established a boat yard at Fountain City, Wisconsin in 1889 to build wooden barges. Then a few years later, when the engineers started to build wing dams on the upper Mississippi River, they opened up a stone quarry up on the bluff above the boat yard. They built a double incline railroad up to the quarry. The loaded cart going down to the boat yard would pull the empty cart up. This boat yard is still very active. It is used to repair equipment and for winter storage during the yearly freeze-up for all the Army Engineers' boats, dredges, and barges.

### Albino Deer

The scenic upper Mississippi River Valley has many joys of beauty, including an occasional deer. Around Fountain City, Wisconsin, you may see an Albino (all white) deer. For proof of this, stop at Fountain City and go into the First State Bank. There in the lobby is a full-mounted Albino buck deer with pink eyes–a rare beauty indeed.

### Land Speculator

After the United States opened up the Louisiana Territory for homesteading, land developers filed claims and bought up claims with the purpose of establishing a town and, of course, make a profit. Most of the developers were very honest businessmen, but not all! One land speculator, land shark would be

*Paddle-Wheel Steamboat "Clyde" loading cord woood onboard while going up the river from a barge tied alongside.*
*Courtesy Winona County Historical Society.*

*U.S. Army Corps of Engineers boat yard at Fountain City, Wisc.*
*Courtesy Winona County Historical Society.*

*White albino deer with pink eyes that can be seen occasionally around Fountain City, Wisconsin. Courtesy Rob Drieslein and Winona Daily News.*

a better name, bought up land in a valley just up the Mississippi River from Winona, Minnesota. He laid out the town of Rollingstone. Then he went back to the state of New York and sold lots in his city of Rollingstone that, according to him, was fully developed with streets, a business district, school, and churches. Four hundred people bought lots.

Then, in the fall of 1860, these new owners got off the paddlewheel steamboat and walked up the valley to see the city of Rollingstone. There was nothing! Not even a road.

Some bought lumber off the rafts going down the river and built homes. Others built sod houses or lived in caves. Many got sick and died that winter. Of those still alive in spring, many left to return to their families still in the state of New York.

### Vertical Merry-go-round
### Ferris Wheel

A small Mississippi River town, Minneiska, Minnesota, was the home of the man who built the first ferris wheel, Mr. Putman Gray. He built it and set it up at the Winona County Fair in 1892. It was an instant success. By rights, it should be called the Putman Wheel. Of course, now Putman Wheel sounds strange. But, in 1892, it wouldn't be any stranger than calling it the Ferris Wheel. Ferris was

*Fountain City, Wisconsin levee.*
*Courtesy Winona County Historical Society.*

a man's name also. How did it happen? Putman called his ride the vertical merry-go-round. At the Winona County Fair in 1892, Mr. G.W.G. Ferris saw Mr. Putman Gray's carnival ride, bought the rights to it, and took it to the Chicago World's Columbian Exposition in 1893. That's when it got the name, Ferris Wheel.

### Steamboat Names a Town

Charles Reed came up the Mississippi River from his trading post at Trempealeau, Wisconsin, to stake a claim on land where the Zumbro River enters the Mississippi. He had the land surveyed and plotted out the village.

Along the river bank laid a sunken paddlewheel steamboat. The pilot house was still above water. Painted on the side of the pilot house was the boat's name, "West Newton". While Charles Reed was standing on the river bank looking at the "West Newton", he thought why not call the village, West Newton. Besides it would save him the cost of a sign. So, in 1853, the village of West Newton was born.

At first, with a boom site close by for rafting logs for the paddlewheel steamboats, the village of West Newton grew. By 1870, it had a hotel, general store, and a post office. But by 1900, log rafting came to an end. With the loss of work, the people moved away.

Now West Newton is a ghost town with just a few summer fishing cottages.

### Lake Pepin

The Chippewa River created Lake Pepin. After thousands of years of the Chippewa River bringing sand into the Mississippi, it built up a large sand bar that held back the water of the Mississippi and created a lake, twenty-two miles long, two miles wide. During the era of the paddlewheel steamboats, Lake Pepin was a favorite stretch for a race.

The Sioux Indians called the lake, "Pen-vee-cha-mday"-lake of mountains.

Father Hennepin, in 1679, was the first white man to see Lake Pepin. The Sioux Indians had taken him prisoner. He was feeling very sorry for himself. He called the lake, "Lac-des-Pleurs"-lake of tears.

While Lake Pepin was part of the French Territory, the French Army (in 1700) built a fort out on a point that extended into the lake which they named, "Point AuSable"-long point. The French Army also named the Lake after an ancient Franks king, "Pepin the Short". The fort on Point AuSable served as home base for the first Christian missionaries on the upper Mississippi River. A chapel was built on Point AuSable in 1727.

Opposite Point AuSable is a bluff on the Wisconsin

*Str. "Favorite", 1859-1868, side-wheel, wood hull, built in Cincinnati, Ohio, for LaCrosse and St. Paul Packet Co., 252 tons. Piloted by Capt. William F. Davidson and his brother. Courtesy Winona County Historical Society.*

shore is the historical "Maiden Rock". An Indian legend gave the bluff its name.

Chief Red Wing's oldest daughter, We-no-nah, was in love with an Indian boy that was a hunter. We-no-nah's parents and brothers decided she should marry an Indian brave that was a warrior. Her family started to make preparations for the wedding ceremony. We-no-nah would have nothing to do with this warrior. Early in the morning, she escaped from their camp and fled to the top of this high bluff overlooking Lake Pepin. Her brother, after discovering her missing, ran after her and tried to stop her. But We-no-nah leapt to her death instead of marrying the warrior.

James "Bully" Wells established a trading post in the bay just above Point AuSable in 1839. The river pilots called his landing, Bully Wells Bay. Bully Wells was married to an Indian half-breed squaw. So he was deeded 100 acres of land where he had his trading post.

Twenty years later, Bully Wells Bay was the village of Frontenac. In 1867, Lakeside Resort Hotel was built here–the first summer resort in Minnesota. The Resort was operated for 72 years. It closed in 1939.

The author of the book, Little House in the Big Woods, Laura Ingalls Wilder, was born along the shore of Lake Pepin near the village of Pepin in Wisconsin on February 7, 1867. Although the original log house and barn in her story are no longer there, a replica of the log house has been built on this historical site with

*Log house replica of author, Laura Ingalls Wilder home where she was born in Pepin, Wisconsin. Courtesy Winona County Historical Society.*

a monument in her memory.

Lake Pepin was the first lake to have water skis used on it. In 1922, an 18-year-old youth, Ralph Samuelson, enjoyed skiing in the winter on the slopes around Lake City, Minnesota. After some experimenting, Ralph bought 2 pine boards, 8 inches wide, 10 feet long for $1.00 each and fashioned the first pair of water skis. They looked like narrow toboggans. To be towed fast enough to get on top of the water, he was towed behind an airplane. Boats in 1922 didn't have the power they do today.

On the upper end of Lake Pepin, there is a bluff on the Minnesota shore. This bluff, to a boater cruising up the lake, looks like a point. But it isn't. It is just a long sweeping bend. It is called Point No Point. A few years before the Wright Brothers successfully flew their airplane, there were flying machine experiments conducted off Point No Point Bluff. None were successful. They all ended up in the bottom of Lake Pepin.

There is a limestone baptismal font in St. John the Divine Church in New York City that came from a quarry up on the bluff of Point No Point.

*A 1966 picture of the "Father of Water Skiing",*
*Ralph Samuelson, holding the water skis he used in 1922.*
*Courtesy Winona County Historical Society.*

## Red Rock

Just above Newport, Minnesota, on the east shore of the Mississippi River, there laid a large piece of red granite, about 4 1/2 feet square. How it got there, no one knows.

Chief Little Crow's tribe of the Sioux Indian nation used this red granite rock as a worshipping altar to the Great Spirit. During the worshipping ceremony, they would place an offering of food on the red granite altar for the Great Spirit.

When Twin City Towing established Barge Fleeting at this site, the red granite rock was removed and placed in the churchyard of the Newport Methodist Church.

Near where this red granite was, there is a Coast Guard Navigation Aid that the river pilots named, Red Rock.

## Virgin Island

Yes, there is a Virgin Island in the Mississippi River. You will find it about 5 miles below St. Paul, Minnesota. A Sioux Indian legend gave this island its name.

Chief Little Crow's daughter and a young Indian brave were deeply in love. A few days before they were to be married, the young brave was killed by a band of Chippewa Indian warriors.

Chief Little Crow's daughter felt very sad over the loss of her husband-to-be. One afternoon, she swam across the river to this island. In the evening, when she hadn't returned, a search party went over to the island to locate her. They found she had, in her grief, hung herself. From that day on, the island was called Virgin Island.

### City Moves

During the 1860's across the Mississippi River from St. Paul, Minnesota, a settlement of Russian-Jewish immigrants got started. By 1870, the settlement was a village large enough to be chartered. It was named West St. Paul. But the city lost its charter a few years later.

What happened was the mayor and city officials of West St. Paul voted themselves such large salaries, they bankrupted the village. When the state government became aware of this, they took West St. Paul's charter away, and the village was absorbed by the city of St. Paul.

Years later, West St. Paul was chartered again. But then, it wasn't along the Mississippi River. That land was now part of the city of St. Paul. West St. Paul is now about 2 miles south of the Mississippi River.

Now, of course, all these communities: West St. Paul, South St. Paul, Mendota Heights, Inver Grove Heights, have all grown together with St. Paul.

### River Song

There are many river songs. "Old Man River" and "Cruising Down the River" are a couple. But there is an old southern folk song that the crews on the paddlewheel steamboats would sing as they carried cotton-bales and freight to and from the levee, "The Levee Song". The chorus goes like this: "I've been working on the levee, all the live long day".

After the paddlewheel steamboats were replaced by railroads, some unknown banjo player changed the word, levee, in the song, to railroad. So, to this day, at sing-alongs, this song is know as "I've Been Working on the Railroad".

But if you give some thought to the rest of the words, it is still about the paddlewheel steamboat, "Dinah" with the Captain asking the boat to blow its horn. I guess a train could be named, "Dinah", but a train has an engineer-not a captain.

# Chapter Twelve
# *River Towns of the Upper Mississippi River*

Cities and Towns From St. Louis, Missouri, to Minneapolis, Minnesota

### St. Louis, Missouri

O n April 9, 1682, French explorer, LaSalle, claimed the Mississippi Valley Territory for King Louis XIV of France. Then, 80 years later, 1762, King Louis XIV gave the territory west of the Mississippi River to his cousin, King Charles III of Spain, to keep the British from taking it.

Pierre Laclede, a French fur trader, in 1764 set up a trading post just below the mouth of the Missouri River on the west bank of the Mississippi River at Short of Bread Village. Laclede changed the name of the village to St. Louis in honor of the French king.

His private landing on the levee was known by the rivermen as Laclede's Landing. The British army attacked the city of St. Louis in 1779, but with help from the Spanish forces, the British were defeated. In 1800, King Charles III of Spain gave the Louisiana Territory back to France. Then on April 30, 1803, the United States made a deal with Napoleon and bought all the French Territory west of the Mississippi.

The paddlewheel steamboat, "Pike", was the first steamboat to make a run up the Mississippi River to St. Louis. It was in the year of 1817 and was piloted by Captain James Reed. With the paddlewheel steamboats coming up the Mississippi River to St. Louis,

*St. Louis, Missouri, river front around 1900. Note the coal barge alongside the Str. "Quincy".*
*Courtesy Murphy Library, U.W.-LaCrosse.*

Missouri, St. Louis became the Gateway to the Northwest. St. Louis was a boom town. In 1840, St. Louis had a population of 16,000. By 1860, it had a population of 160,000, and by 1880 a population of 350,000.

St. Louis had its worst disaster in 1849. The paddlewheel steamboat, "White Cloud", tied off at the levee caught fire. In a short time, 23 paddle-wheel steamboats were ablaze. Soon many of the warehouses on the riverfront were burning. The fire was finally stopped by dynamiting buildings in the path.

Anheuser Busch Brewery started making beer in St. Louis in 1857. Guess where they got the water to make their beer–and still today–the Mississippi River,

about 15 million gallons a day.

The first world's fair to have electricity was in St. Louis in 1904. Also, at this fair, hot dogs and ice cream cones were first introduced.

### Alton, Illinois

The first settlers to come to Alton, Illinois, were French fur traders. They established an Indian trading post here in 1785. But it failed and was disbanded in 1807.

Mr. Rufus Easton, a St. Louis lawyer, in 1817, bought up the land. He plotted lots out and named the village in honor of his son, Alton. The village voted to incorporate into a city in 1837.

Alton, Illinois, was to be the site where the duel of swords between Lincoln and Shields was to take place, but was cancelled. One of the famous Lincoln and Douglas debates took place here in 1858. Just up the river from Alton, Illinois, painted on a limestone bluff face is the historical Indian painting of The Piasa Bird. This was first viewed and recorded by Father Marquette and Joliet in 1673. Reverend Elijah P. Lovejoy, who for 35 years had used his newspaper to crusade against human slavery, was shot and killed here on November 9, 1837, by a hostile mob.

*The PIASA BIRD.*
*A huge Indian painting on the limestone*
*bluff just north of Alton, Ill.*
*Courtesy Winona County Historical Society.*

*Paddle-Wheel Steamboat "Alton" on an excursion cruise.*
*Courtesy Winona County Historical Society.*

*Str. "Davenport", 1860-1876, wood hull, built at California, Pa., 340 tons, 203 x 34.3 x 5.2.*
*It was destroyed by an ice floe at St. Louis, Mo., Dec. 13, 1876.*
*Courtesy Murphy Library, U.W.-LaCrosse.*

### Portage des Sioux

The Indians and the French fur trappers would take this 2-mile portage between the Missouri and Mississippi Rivers because it was 30-35 miles shorter than going around to the mouth of the Missouri River. The Spanish army had a fort built at this site in 1799. In 1812, the American Army occupied this fort. Portage des Sioux is where, in 1815, the leaders of the Fox and Sac Indian tribes signed a treaty with the United States which opened up the territories of Wisconsin and Illinois to homesteading. In return, the U.S. gave the Indians $30,000 in presents, such as beads, knives, axes, cooking pots and pans, etc. Chief Black Hawk claimed that the treaty was invalid because the Indian leaders who signed the treaty did not have the authority to sign, and that American Army officers had given the Indian leaders whiskey so the leaders were drunk when they signed. In the river, on a pier, is a 43 foot statue, Lady of the River, blessing every boat that passes by.

### Grafton, Illinois

This is where the Illinois River enters the Mississippi River.

Father Pere Marquette and Joliet, on their return after exploring the Mississippi in 1673, took the

*Our Lady of the River Shrine, a 43 foot white statue of Madonna blessing the river boats as they pass at Portage Des Sioux, Mo. Courtesy Winona County Historical Society.*

Illinois River route back to Lake Michigan. In 1669, the French explorer, LaSalle, and Father Hennepin came down the Illinois River and entered the Mississippi here. Each went their separate ways–LaSalle down the Mississippi to the Gulf of Mexico, and Father Hennepin up the Mississippi to what is now known as the Twin Cities.

*Str. "Clinton", 1872, built at St. Louis, Mo. for the Northern Line Packet Co., 246.9 x 38.4 x 5.7.*
*Courtesy Winona County Historical Society.*

### Clarksville, Missouri

At first, the rivermen called it Appleton Landing. John Burns settled here in 1800 and built his home here. Two years later, an Indian trading post was established here by Fred Dixon. General William Clark, on his way to Prairie du Chien with his 200 troops, camped here for a day or two. In 1818, President James Monroe gave Governor John Miller a land grant of this land. He plotted out the village and named it in honor of William Clark–Clarksville.

Clarksville was a very fast growing river town. Warren Swan, in 1826, built a horse-powered ferry and operated it on the Mississippi River at Clarksville for many years. George Knightly, a blacksmith, started the first bicycle factory in Missouri here in 1856.

Thirty years later, 1886, Clarksville held the First International Bike Race on the Old Belt Road.

The area still produces a lot of apples. Each year, the 2nd weekend in October, Clarksville has a big apple fest celebration. In Clarksville's early years, they would hold an annual rattlesnake hunt. The biggest hunt recorded 700 rattlesnakes in one day.

### Louisiana, Missouri

In 1804, a group of tobacco farmers from Kentucky made homestead claims here and started growing tobacco. By 1860, there were 14 cigar factories located here in Louisiana. Judge James Stark bought land here in 1816. This was the beginning of the world famous Stark Apple Nursery. Judge Stark was the man who developed the "delicious" apple which is still a popular choice today.

The U.S. Army, during the War of 1812 with the British, built Fort Buffalo. The first railroad bridge built across the Mississippi here at Louisiana, Missouri, was completed in 1872. Two years later, private investors built a wagon toll bridge across the river.

### Hannibal, Missouri

A farmer, Abraham Bird, who lost his whole farm

*Boyhood home and museum of Mark Twain at Hannibal, Mo. Courtesy Walker-Missouri Tourism.*

in the 1811 Earthquake at New Madrid, Missouri, came here in 1818 and staked his homestead claim. Using the Government land grant that he received after he lost his farm at New Madrid, he had the land surveyed out into lots and went down to St. Louis. He set up a land office selling the lots to the settlers coming from the East. Hannibal was a boom town in 20 years. In 1838, the villagers voted to incorporate into a city. Soon Hannibal, Missouri, became a sawmill town. Logs from the great pine forests of Northwestern Wisconsin were floated down the Mississippi River in large rafts. During the sawmill years, 1847 to 1880, 50% of the population was Negro labor working in the sawmills.

*Str. "J.H. Johnson", 1863-1874, wood hull, side-wheel, built at Madison, Ind., 244 x 40.5 x 6, steam engines 26.5 inches in diameter with a 7 foot stroke, 4 boilers. On April 1, 1874, it hit a railroad bridge at Hannibal, Mo. and sank. It was raised and dismantled, machinery was put in the Str. "Golden Eagle". Courtesy Murphy Library, U.W.-LaCrosse.*

Sam Clemens (Mark Twain) in 1839 was 4 years old when his father moved to Hannibal, Missouri, from Florida, Missouri, and opened up his law office here. All the landmarks related to Mark Twain's boyhood and his storybook heroes, Tom Sawyer, Huckleberry Finn, and Becky Thatcher have been restored and are open for public tour.

A group of investors, including Mark Twain's father, Mr. Clemens, built in 1856 the first railroad across the state of Missouri from Hannibal to St. Joseph. Then, in 1862, this railroad company built the first railroad car for handling mail here at their shops at Hannibal, Missouri. The first steam locomotive built west of the Mississippi was built here at the Hannibal and St. Joseph Railroad Shops in 1865. They named it "General Grant".

In the mid 1800's, here in America there was a very active religious group called Millerites. The leader was William Miller in New York City. He decided the world was coming to an end in the year of 1843. There was a large following of Millerites in the Hannibal area. They left their farms, jobs, and homes, and went up to the top of the bluff south of Hannibal wearing white robes made from bed sheets and spent their days praying, anticipating the second coming of Jesus. This is the same bluff that is known as "Lover's Leap" today.

## Quincy, Illinois

Quincy's first settler was John Wood. He erected his log cabin here in 1822. As other settlers started to build their homes on these limestone bluffs above the Mississippi River, the village was first known as "The Bluff", and later as "Gem City", the Jewel of the West.

Quincy was the second city in the Illinois Territory to incorporate. In 1834, the name, Quincy, was selected in honor of President John Quincy Adams.

The next year, 1835, John Wood began construction of his permanent home. It is a fourteen-room mansion. When completed in 1838, it was one of the finest examples of Greek Revival architecture in the Midwest. In 1907, the Historical Society took the mansion over and restored the home of Quincy's founder and Illinois Governor, John Wood.

In the early settler days, Quincy had a law that allowed every family to keep one cow and a calf in town. During this time in the history of Quincy, they had a celebration they called "Calf Town Days". The main attraction was a cow chip throwing contest.

The new highway bridge here at Quincy between the states of Illinois and Missouri is the first cable-stayed bridge built in the United States. It is a German engineer design. The span between the two river piers is 1800 feet. By using the cable-stayed design instead of suspension design, it saved the taxpayers 80 million dollars.

### LaGrange, Missouri

Godfrey Lesieur, a French fur trapper, set up an Indian trading post here in 1795, making LaGrange (French for barn) the oldest town north of St. Louis. By 1830, the settlers in the village decided it was time to draw up a plotting plan, and in 1838, LaGrange was incorporated. President Woodrow Wilson's Vice-President, Tom Riley Marshall, was born here in 1854. He campaigned on the slogan, "What this country needs is a good five-cent cigar."

### Canton, Missouri

In 1827, when the first settler arrived here, they called their little village, "Cottonwood Prairie".

The ferry operation across the Mississippi River goes way back to 1853. It was the ferry, "Lewis-Adams". In 1870, it was replaced with the ferry, "Rose Lee". Then in 1889, the paddlewheel steamferry, "Cantonia", was put into operation. In 1910, the ferry, "Cantonia", caught fire. But it was rebuilt and put back into service. There is a ferry operating out of Canton still today.

### Alexandria, Missouri

After the Chief Black Hawk War of 1832 and Iowa

*LaGrange, Mo., oldest town north of St. Louis, Mo. on the upper Mississippi River. Courtesy Murphy Library, U.W.-LaCrosse.*

Territory was opened for homesteading, the Iowa Governor claimed the Iowa-Missouri border was the Fox River. The Missouri Governor claimed the border was 10 miles further north at the Des Moines River. As this debate went on, the village of Alexandria didn't know if they paid tax to Iowa or Missouri.

Then one day in 1839, a Missouri man was cutting down trees full of honey north of the Fox River. He was arrested by the Iowa Sheriff. The Missouri

Governor sent the Missouri Sheriff to free the Missouri man. The Iowa Sheriff arrested him also. Before it was over, both Governors had called out the militia. The newspapers called it "The Honey War".

The Federal Government settled it in Missouri's favor, and the Des Moines River became the boundary. The village of Alexandria ended up in the state of Missouri.

**Warsaw, Illinois**

In the early days, a fur trader set up an Indian trading post here and sold spunk water liquor to the Indians. The rivermen called this point, "Spunk Point".

In 1814, the U.S. Army built Fort Johnson here. The point was then called Fort Johnson. Then, three

*Paddlewheel steamboat museum at Keokuk, Iowa. Courtesy Winona County Historical Society.*

years later, Major Zachary Taylor was given command of the fort. He rebuilt and enlarged the fort and renamed it Fort Edwards. Now the point was called Fort Edwards. Then, three years later (1820), the village had a vote and selected the name of Warsaw.

A local farmer, around 1830, started cutting hay and selling it to the paddlewheel steamboats to feed all the livestock they were carrying. He always had a large haystack by the landing on the point. The rivermen instead of calling it Warsaw Point, called it Haysaw Point.

In 1844, Thomas Sharp, an editor and publisher, opened up a newspaper business at Warsaw. Because his newspaper printed false statements about the Mormons just up the river at Nauvoo, Illinois, the Mormon leaders, Smith brothers, came down one night and smashed his printing press. This act led to the Smith brothers' arrest and the mob's shooting the Smith brothers.

## Keokuk, Iowa

This town was named in honor of the Sac Indian Chief, Keeokuk. Translated, that name means "Running Fox" or "Watchful Fox". At first the village spelled it the Indian way–with two "E's". Keeokuk.

When the first settlers came in 1820, the village was known as "Rats Row". It is the first and oldest permanent settlement in the state of Iowa. American Fur Company chose this location for a trading post site in 1828.

During a special holiday outing of all the merchants, businessmen, and leaders on the paddlewheel steamboat, "Red Rover", they decided the name, "Rats Row" wasn't a proper name for their village. After a lot of discussion, they settled on the name, Keeokuk. It was Chief Keeokuk who, when the treaty was signed, set aside this corner of the Iowa Territory for the forty-two Indian half-breeds in his tribe. After passed by Congress in 1824, this land was known as "The Half-Breed Tract".

In Rand Park overlooking the river, there is a life-size statue of Chief Keeokuk. This is also the home town of Jane Clemens, Mark Twain's mother.

Before 1877, Keokuk was the transfer point of passengers and freight on the Mississippi River because of the dangerous lower rapids at Keokuk. The paddlewheel steamboats from St. Louis off loaded here and picked up freight that had been off loaded by the paddlewheel steamboats that had brought down freight to the head of the lower rapids. The freight and passengers were transported over land around the rapids first by horse and wagon to the waiting paddlewheel steamboats, and later by a short line railroad. The Army Engineers, in 1866-1877, built a lock and canal system around the rapids which eliminated this transfer.

The largest power plant on the Mississippi River

*Str. "S.S. Thorp", stern-wheel, steel hull, built at Dubuque, Iowa for Federal Barge Lines, 130.1 x 35.1 x 5.1, steam engines 800 H.P.
Courtesy Bert Finch.*

KATE SWINNEY        FEDERAL ARCH        BELLE GOULD        U.S. MAIL

*Keokuk, Iowa Levee.*
*Courtesy Winona County Historical Society.*

was built here in 1910-1913. This dam raised the water and created a lake which submerged the canal system that was built in 1877.

The city of Keokuk has converted the paddlewheel steamboat, "George M. Verity", into a paddlewheel steamboat museum. The Dubuque Shipyard built the paddlewheel steamboat in 1927 for Upper Mississippi Barge Line. They had it named, "Thorp". In 1928, Federal Barge Line took over the operation of the "Thorp". Then, in 1940, the "Thorp" was sold to ARMCO Steel. ARMCO Steel renamed it "Geo. M. Verity" to honor the founder and first President of American Rolling Mills. Twenty years later, 1960, ARMCO Steel decided to retire the paddlewheel steamboat, the "Geo. M. Verity". The city of Keokuk asked to turn the "Geo. M. Verity" into a paddlewheel steamboat museum. ARMCO Steel liked the idea and sold the "Geo. M. Verity" to the city of Keokuk for one dollar.

### Nauvoo, Illinois

Nauvoo is a Hebrew term. Translated it means "beautiful place" or "pleasant land". When it was first settled around 1824, it was the village of "Venus". But by 1834, the nearby village, Commerce, grew and absorbed it. In 1839, Governor Boggs of Missouri signed The Extermination Order to remove the

*Quarry stone home built at Nauvoo, Ill. in 1828 by Capt. James White. This was the first home built in Nauvoo. Capt. James White bought the land to build this home from an Indian chief with 200 sacks of corn. Courtesy Nadine Anderson, Nauvoo, Ill.*

Mormons from Missouri. Joseph Smith, the leader of the Mormon Church, and his fellow church members had to leave the state of Missouri or be shot. They crossed back over the Mississippi River in the winter on the ice and settled in the village of Commerce.

They started building new homes right away. When the city was granted a charter, they selected the name, Nauvoo. The charter they received from the state of Illinois granted Nauvoo autonomous state power to pass any law not in direct conflict with the state or Federal Constitution. By 1844, Nauvoo was the largest city in the state of Illinois with a population of around 20,000. Joseph Smith had his own army of three thousand soldiers. The non-Mormons in Illinois began to fear that the Mormons would take over the state. This led to many false charges

*Early view of Nauvoo, Illinois on the upper Mississippi River. Courtesy Nadine Anderson, Nauvoo, Ill.*

made against the Mormons. A newspaper in town, The Nauvoo Expositor, started printing critical articles against Joseph Smith and his fellow Mormons. The Nauvoo City Council called a meeting. They declared The Nauvoo Expositor a nuisance. That same night, the press was destroyed. The publishers filed a complaint against Joseph Smith and his brother, Hyrum. They were arrested and put in jail. But before they could come to trial, a mob stormed the jail, and the Smith brothers were shot.

The Mormons, then under the leadership of Brigham Young, started leaving the city of Nauvoo for a two-year covered wagon journey to Salt Lake City, Utah. By 1848, Nauvoo was a ghost town. The following year, a group of French settlers resettled the town of Nauvoo. This was a communal group called the Icarians. Things went well for the communal group for a few years, but by 1858, they disbanded.

The Reorganized Church of Jesus Christ of the Latter Days Saints (Mormons) established the Joseph Smith Historical Center at Nauvoo in 1918 and began a reconstruction of the city of Nauvoo as it was during the Joseph Smith days.

Now in the Nauvoo area, there are large vineyards which produce a million pounds of grapes a year making fifty thousand bottles of wine a year. One of the 540 gallon wooden wine casks dates back to the French colony in 1852. The old brewery has been shut down for many years. The beer aging cellars are now used to make blue cheese.

The Browning Gun Manufacturing got its start here in Nauvoo. Jonathan Browning built his home here in 1843. His son, John M. Browning, took up the gunsmith trade and started designing and building guns in his father's home which is still standing here in Nauvoo today.

### Fort Madison, Iowa

In the winter of 1808-1809, the Army built a fort here to protect the trading post that was here. They named the fort in honor of President James Madison. During the War of 1812, Dixon, a British agent, sup-

*Paddlle-Wheel Steamboat "City of Nauvoo" Ferry that operated on the Mississippi River at Nauvoo, Illinois.
Courtesy Winona County Historical Society.*

*Fort Madison, Iowa. Picture of the full scale replica of the fort that was destroyed by fire here in Sept. 1813.*
*It is now open for public tours. The original fort was built by troops of the First U.S.*
*Infantry Regiment under command of Lt. Alpha Kingsley in 1808-1809.*
*Courtesy Fort Madison City Parks.*

plied Chief Black Hawk with weapons and ammunition so Black Hawk and his warriors could attack Fort Madison. Black Hawk laid siege on the fort in 1813. After the fort supply lines were cut off, Lt. Hamilton Small Garrison was greatly outnumbered, out of food, and low on ammunition. The troops set fire to the fort and under cover of darkness, escaped through a trench from the fort to the Mississippi River. They went down the river to St. Louis. After the Black Hawk War, in 1839, Iowa established a penal institution here at Fort Madison. It is the oldest jail west of the Mississippi River.

Fort Madison grew, and in 1847, S.D. Morrison began manufacturing farm tools. About this same time, the Santa Fe Railroad built a bridge across the Mississippi here. The first wooden trestle bridge has been replaced with a riveted steel bridge which has the longest double deck, double track swing span in the world. The upper deck is for cars and trucks. The lower deck is for trains.

*Snake Alley: the most crooked street in the world: 5 half-curves, 2 quarter-curves. Located at Burlington, Iowa. Courtesy Burlington Area Convention and Tourism Bureau.*

### Burlington, Iowa

The city of Burlington has the most crooked street in the world. You will find it listed in Ripley's Believe It or Not. It is called Snake Alley. Snake Alley has five half-curves and two quarter curves over a distance of 275 feet, rising 58.3 feet, in the length of a short city block. All the homes on Snake Alley were built in the 1845-1880 Period.

The Indians called these bluffs and hills, Sho-ko-kon, "Flint Hills". The Indians used the flint to make tools and arrowheads.

Lt. Zebulon Pike, in 1805, on orders to explore and survey the upper Mississippi River, set up a temporary camp here up on the bluff which is now Crapo Park.

*River front levee of Burlington, Iowa.*
*Courtesy Winona County Historical Society.*

*Muscatine, Iowa.*
*Courtesy Muscatine Historical Society.*

This was the first time the American Flag, Stars and Stripes, was raised in the territory that became the state of Iowa.

The early settlers made homestead claims here in 1833. Some came from Burlington, Vermont, and named the village after their home town.

Burlington was the capital of Iowa Territory for three years, 1837-1839. Then the state capital was moved to Iowa City.

The early settlers were farmers and started raising hogs and were very successful at it. Soon the paddlewheel steamboats were landing at Burlington Levee and loading up with barrels of salt pork, smoked hams, and lard. Burlington became known as Porkapolis of Iowa.

### Muscatine, Iowa

Muscatine is the only city in the world with this name. But this landing on the upper Mississippi River had two other names before it became Muscatine, Iowa.

Colonel George Davenport in Rock Island, Illinois, sent his partner, Mr. Farnham, here to set up another trading post in 1833 to trade with the Mascoutin Indian village located just down river–what is now known as Muscatine Island. Two years later, 1835, James W. Casey staked a homestead claim here and started selling cord wood to the paddlewheel steamboats. Now the rivermen called this landing "Casey's Wood Yard". The next year, 1836, Col. John Vanter from Bloomington, Indiana, saw an opportunity here and bought out Col. Davenport's trading post. He had the land surveyed and filed the plotted city and Casey's Wood Yard became Bloomington, Iowa. The following year, Bloomington became the county seat.

Bloomington's mail was getting lost. It was going to Bloomington, Illinois or Indiana. It was decided the

*John F. Boepple came from Germany in 1887, started making buttons from Mississippi River clam shells at Muscatine, Iowa. Courtesy Winona County Historical Society.*

best solution was to change the name of their town. They voted for the name, Muscatine. No other city in the world has that name. Muscatine is an Indian term, translated it means either "fiery nation" or "burning island" or "people of the prairie". Take your pick.

By 1850, Muscatine had its own newspaper owned by Mr. Clemens, Mark Twain's brother. Mark Twain worked for his brother at the newspaper for awhile.

The first passenger train to operate in Iowa was the Mississippi and Missouri Railroad operating a passenger train between Muscatine and Davenport, Iowa in 1855. The major industry in Muscatine from 1860 to 1890 was lumbering. There were two large sawmills here. After all the logs in the area were sawed up, they started bringing them down the Mississippi River in large rafts from northern Wisconsin.

A German, Boepple, was in the button manufacturing business in Germany. He found that the shell from the freshwater Mississippi clam could be made into buttons. In 1881, he packed up everything and immigrated to America. After a few years of searching for a good supply of clams, Boepple decided to set up his button factory at Muscatine in 1890. It was called Hawkeye Pearl Button Factory. Muscatine became known as Pearl Button City.

*George Davenport's home on Arsenal Island and Rock Island, Ill. Courtesy Rock Island Preservation Commission.*

**Davenport, Iowa**

Davenport was called "Stubbs Eddy" by the early rivermen. The Indians called it "Morgan's Camp". It was a favorite campground for Chief Morgan's tribe. Chief Morgan was a half-breed.

The treaty between the United States and the Sac and Fox Indian tribes was signed here after the Chief Black Hawk War of 1832, which opened up the Iowa Territory for homesteading. Antonine LeClaire, an interpreter who spoke English, French, Spanish, and twelve Indian dialects, helped Chief Keeokuk and other of the Sac and Fox Indian tribes negotiate the treaty. For his help, the Indian Chiefs requested Antonine LeClaire be granted claim to the land opposite Rock Island, which is now the town of Davenport.

Two years later, LeClaire sold 7/8 of this land to

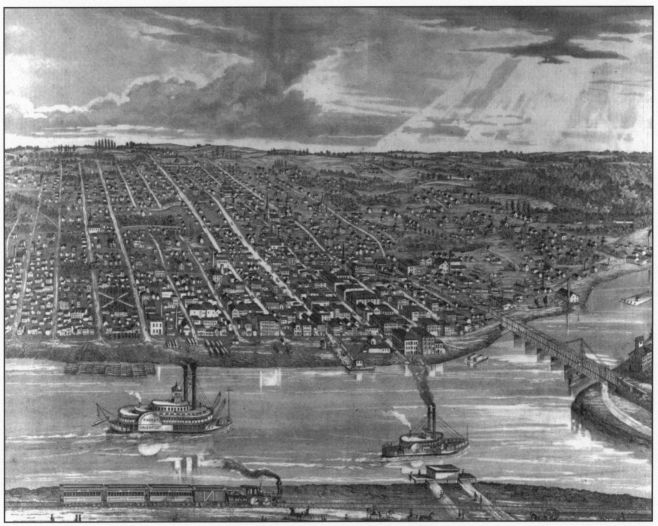

*Davenport, Iowa river front in the late 1890's.*
*Courtesy Murphy Library, U.W.-LaCrosse.*

*Paddle-Wheel Steamboat "W.J. Quinlan" Ferry that operated on*
*the Mississippi River between Rock Island, Illinois and Davenport, Iowa.*
*Courtesy Winona County Historical Society.*

Colonel George Davenport's land development company. They had it surveyed and plotted the city of Davenport.

In 1851, the city of Davenport was incorporated. Then, in 1856, Rock Island Railroad built the first railroad bridge across the Mississippi River here between Davenport and Rock Island. Davenport became a boom town. In four years (1860), Davenport population grew to 20,000. Like Keokuk, Davenport–located just below the upper rapids–during low water was a transfer port for passengers and freight.

### Rock Island, Illinois

This city got its start in 1816 when Colonel William Lawerance with the U.S. Army built Fort Armstrong on Arsenal Island. George Davenport set up a trading post on the island that same year.

After the Black Hawk War of 1832, Russell Farnham, George Davenport's partner, started selling lots and the village of Farnhamsburg got started. In 1835, the town was platted and called Stephenson. In 1841, when the city was chartered, it got its name-Rock Island. When Captain Crawford made his historical paddlewheel steamboat trip up the Mississippi River in 1823 to Fort Snelling, George Davenport helped pilot the "Virginia" up through the Rock Island Rapids.

During the Civil War, Arsenal Island was used as a prisoner of war camp. At times, there were 12,000 Confederate soldiers held there. Almost 2,000 of them died in that prison camp and are buried in a special Confederate cemetery on the Island.

When George Davenport first came here in 1816, he filed claim to 1/4 section of land on Arsenal Island. He paid $1.25 per acre. He built his home there by the river. It has been restored, and is now open for public tours. Twenty-five years later, George Davenport was murdered. In 1867, the U.S. Government bought his 1/4 section for $40,740.00 from his family.

All of Arsenal Island, 946 acres, is U.S. Government property. The U.S. Army builds and tests military equipment on the Island. Four to six thousand civilians are employed in 200 buildings that the Army

*Dred Scott, Dr. John Emerson's slave, who homesteaded the land that is now the city of Bettendorf, Iowa, for the doctor. Courtesy Bettendorf Public Library.*

has there now.

Weyerhauser Lumber Company got its start at Rock Island. Mr. Weyerhauser and his partner, Mr. Denkmann, bought up a burned-out sawmill here. They rebuilt it and started bringing large log rafts down the Mississippi River from northern Wisconsin. Weyerhauser Lumber is one of the biggest lumber producers in the United States.

### Bettendorf, Iowa

This land was homesteaded by the famous slave, Dred Scott. His owner, Dr. Emerson, had Dred Scott homestead this land for the Doctor. This action eventually led to the historical Dred Scott Trial in St. Louis, and was one of the events leading up to the Civil War.

Early settlers called this stagecoach stop, Lillinthal. Then, in 1858, Elias Gilbert bought Dr. Emerson's land, divided it into lots and when the village was charted, it was named Gilbert Town.

The Bettendorf Wagon Company in Davenport needed more room. In 1902, the Gilbert Town officials invited The Bettendorf Company to move to Gilbert Town. Gilbert Town offered them the land they needed and raised $15,000.00 to help build their new plant. One year later, the town was incorporated as Bettendorf, Iowa.

By 1908, the Bettendorf Wagon Company was building railroad boxcars. In the next six years, the Company expanded four times. By 1920, the Bettendorf Company employed three thousand employees and were producing thirty-five boxcars a day.

Hard times during the Depression forced the Bettendorf Company to close its doors. During World War II, the U.S. Government took over the plant. It was known as the Quad Cities Tank Arsenal. After the War, it was sold to the Case Tractor Company.

*Bettendorf Railroad Boxcar Plant.*
*Courtesy Bettendorf Public Library.*

*Paddlewheel steamboat guiding a log raft down the Mississippi River under the old Dubuque Highway Toll Bridge.*
*Courtesy Winona County Historical Society.*

### Moline, Illinois

Early settlers in 1829 called this village Milltown because two men, Spence and Spears, had dammed up the Illinois-Arsenal Island back channel of the Mississippi River using the water power to operate both a sawmill and a flour mill.

Then in 1843, David B. Spears, Spencer White, Joel and Huntington Wells, Nathan Bass and Charles Atkinson filed a plot plan of the city and chose the name, Moline, from the French word "Moulin" meaning "Mills".

John Deere opened his plow factory here in 1848. The plows the pioneers brought with them from the East would not scour in the rich black soil of Iowa. John Deere designed a different shape steel plow that would.

Moline was incorporated in 1872. The Monocoupe Airoplain was built here in the 1920's by Willard Velie, who got started in the late 1880's building carriages and the Velie Autos here. His home, which is now an antique shop and restaurant, was a Mediterranean style mansion of 14 bedrooms and 12 baths.

### LeClaire, Iowa

During the mid 1800's, here along the Mississippi, there were two villages, LeClaire and Parkersburg, with a small crossroad hamlet between them. George Harlan was first to file a claim and build a home here in 1834. Before he was here a year, Eleazer Parkersburg bought him out and started the pioneer settlement village, Parkersburg. Three years later, 1837, Antonine LeClaire, noting the progress of Parkersburg which was located just north of his land, had the village of LeClaire layed out. By 1855, the three communities had grown together. They decided to incorporate as one "Town of LeClaire".

LeClaire was located just above the head of the Rock Island Rapids. There were many paddlewheel steamboats and log rafts that broke up attempting to negotiate these rapids. Although the rapids spelled disaster, it meant something entirely different to the city of LeClaire.

Smith and Suiter, two young men with the help of half-breed Indian friends began studying the rapids—learning its cross currents, eddies, and locating the submerged rocks. It wasn't long before their services as special rapids pilots were in great demand. They were paid well–$10.00 in gold each trip. From 1850 to when the canal was built around the rapids in 1877, there were twenty rapids pilots living in LeClaire. All LeClaire business was connected in one way or another to the river.

Six men from LeClaire have their names in our history books:

*The last Steam paddle-wheel towboat to operate on the Upper Mississippi River.*
*Courtesy Winona County Historical Society.*

James Eads designed and built the famous Eads Bridge at St. Louis, Missouri.

Sam Van Sant was the first to successfully use a paddlewheel steamboat to push log rafts down the Mississippi River. He moved to Winona, Minnesota so he could be closer to log rafting. He also served two terms as Governor of Minnesota.

Thomas Eads, James Ead's son, invented the diving bell.

Buffalo Bill, a Pony Express rider, Army scout, buffalo hunter, and Wild West showman was born here.

Thomas Doughty, a chief engineer on a gun boat in the Civil War, built the first naval periscope, so the pilot could see to navigate while the gunboat was under enemy fire.

James S. Ryan designed, built, and patented "the black box"–the first flight recorder now used on all air lines.

### Clinton, Iowa

Known as "Sawdust Town", in 1835, Elijah Buell filed a claim here and started a ferry operation. Settlers first called the village, New York. Then in 1855, the Iowa Land Division of the Chicago Northwestern Railroad bought Buell's claim and named the town, Clinton. The next year, 1856, the first sawmill was built and "Sawdust Town" got start-

ed. By 1870, Clinton had 12 sawmills producing 100 million board feet a year from logs brought down the Mississippi River in rafts. By 1880, there were 17 millionaire lumber barons living in Clinton, Iowa–the largest producer of lumber in the world.

A very famous movie star and actress was born here in a home at 4th and South in 1861–Helen Louise Leonard. On stage and in movies, she was known as Lillian Russell.

*Paddlewheel steam towboat built in 1936.*
*It towed barges until 1950, now a showboat at Clinton, Iowa.*
*Courtesy Murphy Library, U.W.-LaCrosse.*

Up on the levee of Clinton's city front is a show-boat. This paddlewheel steam towboat was built by Dravo Company in 1936, hull 171.4 x 34.6 feet with compound steam engines. The "Omar" towed coal barges on the Ohio River. In 1950, the "Omar" was sold to the state of West Virginia. The state changed it from a towboat to a showboat and used it in the state's centennial. They named it "Rhododendron", the state's flower. In the late 1960's, Clinton, Iowa, bought it. They built a concrete cradle for it on the

*Savanna, Ill. river front.  Courtesy Carrell County Genealogical Society.*

levee. During a spring flood, it was floated in, and onto its cradle.

### Savanna, Illinois

Council Bluffs is the name the Indians gave the bluff area by Savanna. This was a favorite meeting place for the chiefs of the tribes to come together and iron out their disagreements.

The Racine Mississippi Railroad was the first to extend its tracks to Savanna in 1856. This railroad later became known as the Milwaukee Railroad. Very shortly after, Savanna became a thriving railroad center. At one time, 24 passenger trains a day stopped at Savanna. Now there are none, just freight trains. About 5 miles up the river from Savanna is the U.S. Army's Savanna Proving Grounds.

Wayne King, the famous dance band leader of the 1920's-1930's grew up in Savanna. When he was a small child, he became an orphan, and his aunt living in Savanna raised him. Wayne King graduated from the Savanna High School.

*View of the entrance to the Dubuque, Iowa ice harbor and downtown Dubuque. Captain Ron Larson photo.*

*Steam Paddle-Wheel towboat "Sprague". This was the largest steam paddle-wheel towboat that worked on the Mississippi River. The River Pilots called it the "Big Mama". It was built by the Dubuque Boat and Boiler Works at Dubuque, Iowa. Courtesy Winona County Historical Society.*

### Dubuque, Iowa

Julien Dubuque, a French-Canadian, made an agreement with the local Indian tribe that allowed him to start mining lead in this area in 1788. But it wasn't until 1833 that the town of Dubuque started to grow into one of Iowa's largest cities.

In the beginning, Dubuque was included in the Territory of Wisconsin. During that time, the citizens of Dubuque expected their city would become the state capital of Wisconsin when it became a state.

One of the successful lead miners, Kelly, didn't trust banks, so he buried gold coins in several locations on Kelly's Bluff. Sums of $500 and $1000 in gold coins have been found in different locations since he died.

William A. Ryan, better known as "Hog Ryan", started the meat packing company in Dubuque. He made a fortune during the Civil War supplying pork for the Union Army. Meat packing is still a major business in Dubuque.

In the mid 1880's, the Army Engineers built Dubuque's Ice Harbor–a safe winter harbor for the paddlewheel steamboats. The Ice Harbor was also the site where the Dubuque Boat and Boiler Works was located. They built paddlewheel steamboats.

Just north of the Dubuque Ice Harbor-close to the river-is a large brick building that is the Star Brewery–the only operating brewery in the state of Iowa. The Star Brewery was used in the movie starring Art Carney, "You Can Take This Job and Shove It".

Just past the Star Brewery is a strange-looking chimney. It is not a chimney. It is a shot tower. It was used to make lead shot for muzzle-loading rifles during the Civil War.

The man who got a patent on the paper clip was from Dubuque–John L. Harvey.

The Julien Inn has occupied the corner of Second and Main since 1839. It was remodeled three times: 1854, 1874, 1889. Then in 1913, fire destroyed it. Within a little more than a years' time, it was rebuilt. During the Prohibition Years, the Julien Inn was owned by the notorious bootlegger, Al Capone. When things got too hot for him in Chicago, he would come and hide out at the Julien Inn.

*Stonefield Village and Farm Museum at Cassville, Wisconsin. Courtesy Murphy Library, U.W.-LaCrosse.*

*Cassville, Wisconsin levee in the late 1800's. Courtesy Winona County Historical Society.*

**Cassville, Wisconsin**

General Lewis Cass filed a claim here in 1827. He built a lead smelter and smelted lead ore for the miners. In 1836, a land company surveyed out the village of Cassville and built The Denniston House which was to house the Wisconsin State Legislators when Cassville became the state capital. But the city of Madison was chosen instead. Governor Nelson Dewey, after serving two terms as Governor of

*Guttenberg, Iowa and Lock and Dam 10 on the upper Mississippi River.*
*Courtesy Murphy Library, U.W.-LaCrosse.*

Wisconsin, returned to Cassville in the 1850's. He bought the Denniston House, turned it into a hotel-complete with a ballroom. Then he turned his attention to the development of a 2000-acre estate plantation called "Stonefield". Governor Nelson Dewey's Stonefield Estate has been restored and is now a museum. Stonefield Village and Farm Museum is a living replica of a rural farming community in the late 1800's.

### Guttenberg, Iowa

The French fur traders called this area, "Prairie La Porte", meaning "the door to the prairie".

German settlers started arriving here in 1834. These German immigrants decided to honor the German inventor of the first printing press with moveable type–Johann Gutenberg. The name was spelled with 2 "t's" when the city plat was filed.

The Western Settlement Society of Cincinnati helped colonize the town in 1845 with German immigrants. The library in Guttenberg has a facsimile copy of the Gutenberg Bible on display for the public to see.

### Prairie du Chien, Wisconsin–McGregor and Marquette, Iowa

"Prairie du Chien" is French meaning "Chief Big Dog's Prairie". This is the oldest settlement on the upper Mississippi River because this is where the Wisconsin River, which was part of the French Empire Trade Route, enters the Mississippi River.

Each spring, hundreds of Indians would come here to Chief Big Dog's Prairie, set up camp, exchange stories about happenings of the last year, and trade furs–in early years with the French and then, after the War of 1812, with the American Fur Company.

Hercules Dousman took over management of the trading post in 1826. He became Wisconsin's first millionaire, investing in real estate, paddlewheel steamboats, and railroads. Four years after his death in 1872, his wife, Mrs. Dousman and their only son, Hercules II, built a grand mansion, "Villa Louis". The "Villa Louis" is now open to public tours.

During the War of 1812, the British with the help of some Indian warriors, occupied Prairie du Chien. After the War of 1812, the British left, and the U.S. Army rebuilt the fort and named it Fort Crawford. Zachary Taylor was commander at Fort Crawford from 1829 to 1837. At the same time, Jefferson Davis served here and married Zachary Taylor's daughter.

Dr. William Beaumont, a military surgeon, served here in the 1830's. Dr. Beaumont is famous for his experiments that gave us knowledge of our digestive system. The infirmary at Fort Crawford is now a Historical Museum of Surgery.

*Dousman House, Prairie du Chien, Wisconsin.*
*This railroad hotel and residence was built by*
*Hercules Dousman around 1865 on the East River channel.*
*It is now listed on the National Historic Register.*
*Courtesy Griff William's Collection.*

they would hold a penny circus in their back yard with their pet squirrels, raccoons, dog, cats, and rabbits. In 1882, they put a real circus on the road, "The Greatest Show on Earth".

The first woman to receive a degree in dental surgery opened her office in McGregor in 1862.

*Dousman grand mansion built in 1872, located at Prairie du Chien, Wisconsin. Courtesy Griff William's Collection.*

Across the river are two river towns divided by a sandstone bluff, McGregor and Marquette, Iowa. McGregor was the first village to be settled. It started as a ferry landing in 1837. Alexander McGregor was the ferry operator. In 1874, the railroad built a floating pontoon bridge across the Mississippi on the other side of the sandstone bluff. This was the beginning of North McGregor. In 1940, North McGregor changed the name to Marquette.

August Ringling moved to McGregor in 1860 and opened up a harness shop. His famous sons were born here. While they were just youngsters, in the summer,

### LaCrosse, Wisconsin

During the mid-1700's, French fur traders stopped here at this prairie along the banks of the Mississippi River, making trades with Winnebago Indians for furs. The young braves were playing a ball game. The

*This is a picture of the floating railroad bridge that was built across the Mississippi River at Prairie du Chien, Wisconsin, in 1874. Note the large log raft the paddlewheel steamboat is taking through the bridge with the help of a bowboat.*
*Courtesy Winona County Historical Society.*

French called the game, lacrosse, and named the area, "Prairie of Lacrosse". The name got shortened to LaCrosse by the Prairie of Lacrosse postmaster. At that time, the postmaster had to cancel the stamps by hand–by writing by hand the name of the town across the stamp. He got tired of writing that long name each time.

*This historical bronze cannon, cast in Seville, Spain, 1787, is in LaCrosse, Wisconsin Riverside Park. Courtesy Murphy Library, U.W.-LaCrosse.*

Both the Black River and the LaCrosse River join the Mississippi at the same place here at LaCrosse. The Winnebago Indians had a legend about three rivers. Where three rivers meet, tornadoes will never touch down.

Nathan Myrich, the founder of the village of LaCrosse, was only 19 years old when he canoed up the Mississippi River from Prairie du Chien and built a cabin on Barron's Island (Pettibone Park) in 1841. He began trading with the local Indians and selling wood to the paddlewheel steamboats. The next year, 1842, he moved across the river and laid out the village, "Prairie of Lacrosse".

Two important events occurred here in 1858: the railroad reached LaCrosse, and Gottlieb Heileman and his partner, John Gund, founded "G. Heileman Brewery". In its early history, LaCrosse, at one time, had five breweries. The G. Heileman Brewery is the only one still making beer in LaCrosse.

Two paddlewheel steamboats were lost at LaCrosse, Wisconsin. The first one was the "War Eagle". It burned and sank in 1870. Six years later as the shipyard was hauling the paddlewheel steamboat, "Phil Sheridan" out for repairs, the cradles let go and punched large holes in the hull . The boat slipped back into the river and sank. All they could salvage was the machinery.

On LaCrosse's city front levee "Riverside Park", there is an historic bronze muzzle loading cannon. This bronze cannon was cast in Seville, Spain in 1787 for King Charles III. In the mid 1800's, Spain shipped the cannon to Havanna, Cuba to be used in Havanna's defense during the Spanish American War of 1898. It was one of the cannons that took part in the sinking of

*City of LaCrosse, Wisconsin river front about 1901. Courtesy Winona County Historical Society.*

the U.S.S. Maine.

French Island, now a part of the city of LaCrosse, in the 1860's was known as "Saw Mill City". The first sawmill got started in 1852. Logs were floated down the Black and LaCrosse Rivers each spring. By 1880, there were 13 sawmills on French Island employing 3500 men.

More registered river captains lived in LaCrosse than in any other city north of St. Louis in the late 1860's.

There is a breath-taking view of the Mississippi Valley from LaCrosse' 600 foot "Grandad Bluff". It also overlooks the majestic bluffs of Minnesota and Iowa.

**Trempealeau, Wisconsin**

When Father Hennepin was exploring the upper Mississippi River in 1684, he saw large herds of buffa-

*Quarry stone remains of the Melchoir Hotel and Brewery built in 1857 along the riverbank at Trempealeau, Wisconsin. Courtesy Winona County Historical Society.*

*Mount Trempealeau, located about 20 miles up the river from LaCrosse, Wisc. above the river village, Trempealeau, Wisc. Courtesy Winona County Historical Society.*

lo in this valley. In his notes, he called it "Valley of Wild Bulls". The last of the buffaloes in this valley was shot in 1832.

One hundred and sixty years after Father Hennepin was here (1846), Reed filed a claim and built his cabin here. He started trading with Winnebago Indians. The river pilots called it, "Reed's Landing". The settlers called their village,"Montaville". But those names didn't last long. 1856 was a boom year for the village. The price of lots went from $40 to $60 to $1000 each. It was decided to name the town after the mountain: LaMontagne qui Trempealeau, a French name meaning "the mountain which walks in the water". The new hardy Norwegian and German settlers quickly shortened it to Trempealeau.

The Melchoir Hotel and Brewery, a two-story quarry stone building was built in 1857. The brewery soon became a major industry in Trempealeau. Many barrels of beer were shipped by paddlewheel steamboat to cities up and down the river. Now all that remains is the quarry stone walls along the river bank. Up the river bordering the city of Trempealeau is Perrot Park. Here the Trempealeau River enters the Mississippi River, and you find Mount Trempealeau. The French used the Winnebago Indian name for this mountain, "Hay-Nee-Ah-Chah" meaning "mountain whose foot is bathed in water". This is the only mountain on the Mississippi River.

*City of Winona, Minn. river front around the year 1905 with the Str. "J.S." going by.*
*Courtesy Winona County Historical Society.*

*Winona, Minn. river front with the paddlewheel steamboat museum, "Wilkie" in Levee Park.*
*Courtesy Winona County Historical Society.*

When this was French territory, the French Army had a fort on this mountain. The Winnebago Indian tribe have a sacred burial ground on Mount Trempealeau that is still is use today.

### Winona, Minnesota

This sand prairie was known as Chief Wa-ba-sha's Prairie. Much of the Wa-ba-sha tribe's day-to-day and ceremonial life took place in what today is downtown Winona.

When the Sioux Indian nation signed the treaty with the United States in 1851, it opened the Minnesota Territory for homesteading. Captain Orrin Smith landed his paddlewheel steamboat at Chief Wa-ba-sha's Prairie and put off some crew members. They filed a homestead claim. In two years, that homestead was a village of 300 settlers. They called their little village, the village of Montezuma. By 1857, the village of Montezuma had grown to a population of 3,000. They had their own bank, three churches, a flour mill, two sawmills, and wagon and carriage shops. The village voted to incorporate and chose the Indian name We-no-nah, which means, "Chief's first-born daughter". But when the papers were filed, they spelled the name wrong–"Winona".

John Laird arrived in 1855. He bought some riverfront land and started a sawmill. The logs came down the Mississippi River in large rafts. This was the parent company of United Building Centers, that now have dealers throughout the Midwestern states.

In 1859, the citizens of Winona raised $7,000 to start the first teachers college in the state of Minnesota. It was called, Normal School. Now it is Winona State University.

*Paddle-Wheel Steamboat "General Allen".*
*Courtesy Winona County Historical Society.*

Joseph R. Watkins got his start in 1868 making liniment and a patented medicine he called, Egyptian Stick Salve. He travelled the countryside in a horse and buggy selling his salve and liniment. In 1885, he built a factory in Winona, producing personal care products and many different spices-packaging under the Watkins label. The Watkins Company now has over 40,000 dealers throughout the United States.

By 1870, Winona was the third largest city in the state of Minnesota.

Winona has the most beautiful city riverfront park on the Mississippi River. Upon the levee is the "Wilkie". It is an historical steamboat museum, a replica of a

*Alma, Wisconsin, during the log rafting years of 1870-1910.*
*Courtesy Sherman House, Alma, Wisc.*

paddlewheel steamboat that is open for public tours.

One of the bluffs overlooking the city is Sugar Loaf Bluff. This bluff was used as a lookout by Chief Wa-ba-sha's tribe. It has been preserved as an historical site.

### Alma, Wisconsin

Two Swiss bachelors filed a claim here in 1848. They started a wood yard selling cord wood to the paddlewheel steamboats. The river pilots called the

*Boom site where logs that came down the Chippewa River were caught, sorted, and assembled into rafts. Located just above Alma, Wisc. in Beef Slough. Courtesy Winona County Historical Society.*

landing, "12 Mile Bluff". It is 12 miles from here to Lake Pepin. More Swiss immigrants came in 1851. In 1885, this Swiss village of Alma was incorporated.

Alma occupies a narrow strip of land nestled between the Mississippi River and the bluff rising to 500 feet. The city is only two blocks wide and seven

*Wabasha, Minnesota river front.*
*Courtesy Winona County Historical Society.*

*A busy boatyard at Wabasha, Minnesota in 1890. Courtesy Winona County Historical Society.*

*Steam Paddle-wheel Towboat "Aquila". Built at the Boat Works at Wabasha, Minnesota. Courtesy Winona County Historical Society.*

miles long. Most of the buildings on Main Street are over 100 years old and listed with The National Register of Historical Places. Each summer Alma celebrates, "Swiss Heritage Days".

Just up the river from Alma, Beef Slough, was a large logging boom site. Here all the logs that were cut along the Chippewa River were floated down to this site. They were sorted by their brand, rafted together, and taken down the Mississippi River to their owner's sawmill. In the early spring, there would be up to 1500 loggers working here in the years, 1860-1900.

Buena Vista Bluff Park has the most spectacular view of the Mississippi River Valley. The main channel of the Mississippi River passes by at the base of the bluff.

### Wabasha, Minnesota

Augustin Rocque, a Scotch-French Canadian, started a fur trading post here in 1826.

In 1842, a Catholic priest was given a log building in Mendota, Minnesota, to be used as a church in Wabasha. He had it floated down the Mississippi River on a log raft to this landing. He off loaded it here and had it rebuilt on the riverbank. The settlers started to move in. By 1843, the landing became the village of Wabasha. The village was plotted in 1854 and incorporated in 1858.

*Minnesota's oldest operating hotel,*
*The Anderson House, built in 1856 at Wabasha, Minn.*
*Courtesy Wabasha Chamber of Commerce.*

That was the same year Mr. Hurd bought land on the corner of Main and Bridge and built his hotel. In 1901, Grandma Ida Anderson from the Amish colonies in Lancaster, Pennsylvania, took over the hotel, and its been known as the Anderson Hotel ever since. This is the oldest hotel in the state of Minnesota still in operation. Grandma Anderson quickly became famous for her Dutch cooking, which continues today under the direction of her great grandson, John Hall. This 52-room country inn has retained the Victorian customs and tradition of the late 1800's.

The Wabasha Flour Mill got started in 1882. In 1918, the operator of the mill built a road across the river through the Nelson backwater bottoms and installed a current-operated cable ferry. This doubled the trading area of Wabasha.

Thirteen years later, 1931, private investors built a toll bridge across the Mississippi River. It was a very narrow bridge, only 19 feet wide. But it was used until 1988 when it was replaced with the new bridge.

### Red Wing, Minnesota

Chief Red Wing's tribe controlled this territory. His braves called him, "Koo-poo-hoo-sha" (Scarlet Wing) because he wore a swan's wing dyed red in his ceremonial headdress.

The large limestone bluff here on the riverbank was named by the French voyageurs: "LaGrange" which means "The Barn".

In 1835, a Swiss missionary came and spent four years with these Dakota Indians. Then, in 1848, a mission station was built here. Shortly after, pioneer farmers of Scandinavian descent arrived. By 1851, Red Wing had a post office. In 1857, the village was incorporated. By 1873, Red Wing was one of the major wheat exporters in the United States.

Red Wing Stoneware Company, the parent company of Red Wing Pottery, using local sources of red

*Red Wing, Minnesota. 1868 view with the Mississippi River and "Barn Bluff" in the background. Note the Octagon House in lower right center. Courtesy Goodhue County Historical Museum.*

clay, began producing brick, tile pipe and pottery in 1877.

Red Wing, of course, is the home of the nationally known Red Wing boot and shoes.

In 1874, eleven Red Wing businessmen formed a stock company and had the St. James Hotel built. When completed, the St. James Hotel was the most elegant west of Chicago. After 100 years, the St. James Hotel, although structurally sound, was in need of many repairs to bring it back to its Victorian elegance. In 1975, the Red Wing Shoe Company bought the hotel. After extensive restoration and expansion, the Red Wing Shoe Company reopened the doors of the St. James Hotel.

The St. James Hotel now has besides its 60 individually decorated Victorian guest rooms, three restaurants and an exciting gift shop section. This gift shop

*The St. James Hotel was built in 1874 on the river front at Red Wing, Minn. Courtesy Goodhue County Historical Museum.*

section has shops offering clothing, books, antiques, arts, hobby items, cheese, and candy.

Red Wing's Professor Alexander P. Anderson developed the process that is used to produce puffed wheat and puffed rice. Doctor Anderson's estate was given to the Red Wing Technical College.

### Hastings, Minnesota and Prescott, Wisconsin

The St. Croix River joins the Mississippi River here. During the years 1850 to 1916, 25 billion board feet of log and lumber that had been cut from the pine forests of the upper St. Croix River Valley entered the Mississippi River here in large rafts on their way to many of the towns down river.

*Hastings, Minnesota, 1949 river front showing the famous spiral bridge. Courtesy Preservation Commission of Hastings, Minn.*

This was Dakota Indian tribe territory of the Sioux Indian nation. The Chippewa Indians, being pushed west by the English and French, moved into this area. Of course, this led to war between the two tribes. The Chippewa had rifles. The Dakotas only had bow and arrows. A surprise attack in 1755 by the Chippewa invaders in the Prescott area killed 355 Dakotas.

In 1829, Philander Prescott started a trading post here. Fur trappers came down both the St. Croix and Mississippi Rivers and met here each spring. Soon the river pilots called it, "Prescott's Landing". Mr. Prescott also operated a ferry on the St. Croix.

By 1858, the paddlewheel steamboat, "Equator", was making three trips a week from Prescott to Taylor Falls bringing supplies to the sawmills, logging camps, and Scandinavian farmers that had homesteaded in the St. Croix Valley.

Across the Mississippi is the town of Hastings,

*Spiral Highway bridge over the Mississippi River at Hastings, Minn., removed in 1951 after 55 years of use.*
*Courtesy Winona County Historical Society.*

*Prescott, Wisc. where the*
*St. Croix River joins the Mississippi River.*
*Courtesy Winona County Historical Society.*

Minnesota. It was known to the Dakota Indians as "O-wo-bop-te" which means "where turnips are found".

In the fall of 1819, Lt. Oliver and his troops were sent here to guard provisions that were delayed by river conditions. They set up an army post here in a grove of trees along the river. This landing was known as Oliver's Cove until 1853.

Four men, including Minnesota's first Governor, Henry Hastings Sibley, Henry G. Bailly, Alexis Bailly and Alexander Fairbault were major landowners here. When they filed the surveyed plot of the village, to select a name they put their names in a hat. Hastings was the one drawn. In 1857, Hastings was incorporated.

In 1854, Fairbault sold his interest to William G. LeDuc, a lawyer and businessman who, two years later, bought the Gardner Flour Mill that Harrison G. Graham had started in 1853. LeDuc also organized the Hastings and Dakota Railroad in 1866. His home that he had built in 1865, the LeDuc Mansion, is listed in the National Register of Historical Places.

At one time, Hastings had a unique spiral highway bridge across the Mississippi River. It was built in 1894-95 and opened for use on April 27, 1895. It served Hastings for 55 years. In 1951, it was replaced by the present bridge. The citizens of Hastings were so proud of their spiral bridge, they erected a special monument to the spiral bridge in 1976.

### St. Paul, Minnesota

Lt. Pike, on his search for the source of the Mississippi River in 1805, stopped off at the Sioux Indian camp located where the Minnesota River joined the Mississippi River. After a few days of negotiations and smoking a peace pipe, Lt. Pike bought 100,000 acres of the surrounding land for $200 in knives, beads, mirrors, and whiskey. Now this land is part of the Twin Cities–Minneapolis and St. Paul.

St. Paul was "Pigs-Eye Landing" in the early

*1859 view of St. Paul's river front.*
*Courtesy Winona County Historical Society.*

1800's. Pigs-Eye, a one-eyed fur trader and bootleg-ger operated out of a cave in the bluffs along the Mississippi River.

In 1841, a mission station was established here by a Jesuit group dedicated to the Apostle, St. Paul. From then on, it was St. Paul Landing.

*St. Anthony Falls 1859. The river front of Minneapolis, Minn. in the foreground and the city of St. Anthony across the river.*
*Courtesy Winona County Historical Society.*

Captain Louis Robert built the first home in St. Paul. Robert Street was named in his honor. He served as Captain on two paddlewheel steamboats, "Greek Slave" and "Time and Tide".

During the 1840's, there was a steady influx of immigrants arriving by paddlewheel steamboats. By 1849, when St. Paul was selected territorial capital of Minnesota, St. Paul had a population of 649. When the city was incorporated in 1854, St. Paul had reached 10,000.

James J. Hill, in 1856, began building the Great Northern Railroad from St. Paul to the West Coast. In 28 years, 1884, St. Paul was a major railroad center with a population of 100,000.

## Minneapolis, Minnesota

The French missionary, Father Hennepin, was the first explorer to see St. Anthony Falls, which still has the name he gave it.

Just down the river from the falls, built on a commanding bluff overlooking the Minnesota and Mississippi River Valleys, is Fort Snelling. The U.S. Army built this fort in 1819. Fort Snelling has been restored–with black powder, muzzle loading cannons and muskets. It is staffed with officers and soldiers dressed in uniforms of that 5th Army regiment of 1820. Fort Snelling is open for public tours from May through October.

By 1838, on the east bank of St. Anthony Falls, there was a water-powered flour mill, and a small village, St. Anthony. A short time later, there was a like flour mill on the west bank. By 1849, on the west bank was a growing village. Using an Indian and Greek term combined, they named their village: Minne (Indian for water) and Polis (Greek for city), Minneapolis.

With the rich wheat farms nearby, Minneapolis became the largest milling center of the world. Minneapolis is where both General Mills and Pillsbury got their start.

In 1872, the two cities on both sides of the falls became one, Minneapolis. Since then, both Minneapolis and St. Paul have grown together and are now known as the Twin Cities.

**Riverman's Psalm**

The Lord is my Guardian
  I shall not want.
He guides me as I push barges
  up and down the river.
He leads me to the main channel
  He restores my faith
He brings me safely into locks
  and through bridges
For His name sake.

Even though I push barges
  through storm and dark of night
I fear no grounding
  for Thou art with me.

Thy word and Holy Spirit
  they comfort me
Thou provides safe mooring for me
  when we lose power.
Thou watches over my family and
home
  while I am working on the river

Surely goodness and mercy
  shall follow me all the days
  of my life
And I shall dwell in the house
  of the Lord Forever.

                Amen

## A

## B

**G**

# T

# U

# V

# W

**Y**

**Z**

# ORDER FORM

**Qty.**                                                       **Amount**

**HARD COVER** (8½ x 11)
UPPER MISSISSIPPI RIVER HISTORY
_____ Numbered Collectors Edition        **Special** $39.95 _____
(While Limited Supplies Last)

**SOFTBOUND** (8½ x 7½)
_____ UPPER MISSISSIPPI RIVER HISTORY    $18.70 _____

**HARD COVER** (9¼ x 12¼)
_____ STEAMBOATS ON THE FOX RIVER    $29.95 _____

**POCKET BOOKLET** (4 x 7)
_____ RIVER TOW BOAT DECK HAND MANUAL    $7.95 _____

**COLORED PRINT** (13½ x 21 Image Size)
_____ Paddle-Wheel Steamboat J.M. WHITE    $20.00 _____

**BELT BUCKLE**
_____ Paddle-Wheel Steamboat J.M. WHITE    $15.00 _____
(Cast in pewter with color enameled finish)

                                          **Subtotal** _____
On above items MN res. pay 6.5 sales tax_____
**Shipping and Handling** First Item    $3.50
Each Additional Item add $ .75_____
**TOTAL**_____

Check enclosed for $ _____

Please Print Clearly _____

Name _____

_____

Address_____

City_____

State _____Zip _____

**STEAMBOAT PRESS**
1286 Lakeview Ave.
WINONA, MN 55987
Phone 507-452-6018
Fax 507-453-9056